189 Best Bee

Recip

Brewing the World's Best Beer at Home

Book 2

"You will be rewarded by having the experience of tasting some of the world's most unique, and delicious beer available only to an elite few... " Let the party begin!"

By: George Braun

TABLE OF CONTENTS

PUBLISHER'S NOTES

This book is a Reprint

Disclaimer

This publication is intended to provide helpful and informative material. The author and publisher specifically disclaim all responsibility for any liability, loss or risk, personal or otherwise, which is incurred as a consequence, directly or indirectly, from the use or application of any contents of this book.

Any and all product names referenced within this book are the trademarks of their respective owners. None of these owners have sponsored, authorized, endorsed, or approved this book.

Always read all information provided by the manufacturers' product labels before using their products. The author and publisher are not responsible for claims made by manufacturers.

Paperback Edition
Speedy Publishing, LLC
40 E. Main Street, #1156
Newark, DE 19711
This book is a reprint.

DEDICATION

This book is dedicated to all those who want to learn the secret recipes of the world's best beer and to brew these gifts from the gods in the comfort of home. You adventurous beer makers will be rewarded for your efforts by having the experience of tasting some of the world's unique, delicious beer available only to an elite few... of course, you can share the experience with special friends!

(If you are a beginner beer brewer, I recommend that you grab a copy of Charlie Papazian's <u>The Complete Joy of Home Brewing</u>; he is my "go to guy" for basic instructions).

Happy Brewing!

George Braun

P.S. If you would like to have ALL of my secret recipe collection , go ahead and pick up my other book:

451 Best Beer Brewing Recipes:
Brewing the World's Best Beer at Home
Book 1

Chapter 1- BARLEYWINE

All Grain Barleywine

Category Barleywine
Recipe Type All Grain

Fermentables
12 lbs. German Pils malt
3 lbs. Belgian Munich malt
12 oz. British Chocolate malt
2 lbs. British Medium Crystal malt

Hops
1 oz. Eroica (60 min)
2 oz. Northern Brewer (60 min)
1 oz. Kent Goldings (30 min)
.5 oz. Kent Goldings (20 min)
.5 oz. Kent Goldings (finish)

Other
Irish Hops at 15 min

Yeast, Dry Champagne Yeast (secondary)

Procedure The amount of grain here maxed out my bucket turn sparger. The alcohol here is only about 9%, but then I sparged only enough water to accumulate about 6 gallons for the boil. Sparging for an 8 or 9 gallons and then reducing to around 6 gallons when adding the hops should add a boost to the alcohol content. Also, the Irish ale yeast brought the fermentation down to the final gravity. The champagne yeast brought no further fermentation and could be eliminated. Brewed as a single decoct. Strike temp of 144. Main mashes at 154.

Barleywine 2

Category Barleywine
Recipe Type All Grain

Fermentables

10 lbs. DWC (DeWolf-Cosyns Belgian) Pilsener malt
8 lbs. DWC Pale malt
1.5 lbs. DWC CaraVienne malt
0.1 lb. Roasted Barley
0.5 lbs. DWC (Belgian) Munich malt

Hops

2 oz. Northern Brewer pellets (9%) 60 min
1 oz. BC Kent Goldings plugs (5%) 30 min
1/2 oz. BC Kent Goldings plug (5%) 15 min
1/2 oz. BC Kent Goldings plug (5%) 5 min
1/2 oz. Fuggles plug (4.3%) 5 min

Yeast London ale yeast

Procedure Mash schedule:
Mash-in with 10qts @ 42C for a strike temp of 39C
20 minute beta-glucan res
Add 10 quarts at 100C (boiling) to raise to 62C (aiming for 60C),
30 min. beta-amylase rest
Add 6 quarts @ 100C to raise to 67C (aiming for 70C)
1:15 alpha-amylase rest

Take first running (drain all liquid from the mash turn without adding any further sparge water (*)) to get about 4-4.5 gallons @ 1.080. Boiling down to 3 gallons will give an OG of 1.105 - 1.120.

Whirlpool, let settle for 15 minutes and siphon through the counter flow chiller with aerating cane on end.

Pitch yeast slurry from a previous batch of Mild (probably Yeast Lab London Ale (it's a long story)). (By the way, this is my favorite way to pitch *enough* yeast for a Barleywine.) Fermentation was active in 2 hours. The primary was about 2 months @ 65-70F, and dropped from 1.105 to 1.038.

Rack into secondary and add 1 oz. of EKG plugs for dry hopping.

Bottle about 1 month later. Added new yeast, but no priming sugar.

(*) You can (I did) add more hot water to the remaining mash, and sparge out about 7 gallons more wort to make a Bitter at about 1.045.

Barleywine 3

Category Barleywine
Recipe Type Extract

Fermentables
12 lbs. Dry, pale malt extract
.5 lbs. Honey
1 lb. Dry, light malt extract
1.5 lbs. Corn sugar

Hops
2 oz. Chinook boiling hops (13.2 alpha)
2 oz. Cascade boiling hops (5.5 alpha)
2 oz. Fuggles hops (finish)

Other
2 tsp. Irish moss
2 tsp. Sparkeloid

Yeast champagne yeast
Procedure Boil malt, boiling hops, and corn sugar in 1-1/2 gallons water for about 1 hour. In last 30 minutes, add Irish moss, Fuggles, and sparkeloid. Add to 3-1/2 gallons cold water in fermenter. Pitch yeast and ferment about 7 months. Bottle and age.

Barleywine 4

Category Barleywine
Recipe Type Extract

Fermentables
2 cans Munton & Fison Light Malt Extract
2 lbs. Munton & Fison light dried malt extract
. 25 lbs. Domino light brown sugar

Hops
3--1/2 oz. Fuggles hops
.5 oz. Fuggles for finishing

Yeast 2 packs Munton & Fison ale yeast
Procedure We did a single stage fermentation, so I can't answer your question about how long to age in secondary. We gave the finishing hops 10 minutes. As far as conditioning in bottles---well, it's been 14 months now and it keeps getting better. At 2 months it was OK, but cloudy enough that we thought we should have used gypsum. It was also VERY sweet, but also very hoppy and quite smooth. By 9 months it was clear, but quite heavy and we thought maybe less sugar. Last week it had gotten considerably drier and VERY clear. It's really good now, so I don't know if it'll last long enough for me to give you an update later.
Submitted by: Ann Nelligan,

Barleywine Batch 25

Category Barleywine

Recipe Type All Grain

Fermentables
20 lbs. Lager malt
.5 lbs. Crystal malt
5 lbs. Munich malt
1 lb. Roasted lager malt

Hops
1 oz. Goldings leaf hops (5.6% alpha)
1 oz. Hallertauer
.5 oz. Hallertauer
.5 oz. Hallertauer

Other
2 tsp gypsum
. 75 tsp Irish moss in last 10 minutes of boil

Yeast Whitbread ale yeast
Procedure 1 hour 15 minute protein rest at 132 --- 115F.
Mash at 152F with 1/2 ounce amylase enzyme for 2--1/2
hours. Mash out at 165--172. Sparge with 168 water to make
11 gallons. Boil, adding hops as noted. Cool and pitch yeast.
Rack after 1 week, bottle a week later priming with corn
sugar.

Barleywine Batch 29

Category Barleywine
Recipe Type All Grain

Fermentables
10 lbs. Schreier 2--row malt
5 lbs. Munich malt
1 lb. Wheat
. 75 lbs. Crystal malt

Hops

3 lbs. Glenbrew hopped scotch bitter
2.5 oz. Fuggles hops (plug)
1 oz. Hallertauer hops (leaf)

Other
1/5 tsp salt
.5 tsp epsom salt
1 tbsp gypsum

Yeast Belgian ale yeast

Procedure Add salt and gypsum to 4--1/2 gallons 145 water
to make a mash at pH 5.3. Protein rest at 126--120 for 30
minutes. Mash at 153 for 2 hours 50 minutes. Mash out at
165--170. Sparge to make 8--1/2 to 9 gallons wort. Add
Glenbrew extract and boil 90 minutes. Add 1/2 ounce Fuggles
and 1/2 ounce Hallertauer 15 minutes into boil. Add another
1/2 ounce Hallertauer and 1 ounce Fuggles for the last 40
minutes. In the last 10- -15 minutes, add remaining hops.
Chill and pitch yeast. Ferment at 65-- 70F for 6 weeks. Bottle,
priming with corn sugar.

Blind Squirrel Barleywine

Category Barleywine
Recipe Type Extract

Fermentables
6 lbs. Williams light Australian syrup
1 lbs. 10-L crystal---steeped
1 lb. 40-L crystal---steeped

Hops
3 oz. Chinook pellets aa%13 (60 min)
.5 oz. CFJ-90 pellets aa%9 (5 min)
.5 oz. CFJ-90 (dry hopped in secondary)

Other

5 lbs. Williams light Australian dry
1 tsp gypsum at start of boil
1 tsp Irish moss (30 minutes)

Yeast Whitbread dry ale yeast
Procedure Primary fermentation - glass for 5 days at 65 degrees. Secondary in glass for 16 days at 65 degrees. The wort was boiled in 4 gal. pot (3 1/2 volume) with 2 gal. water added to the primary fermenter.

Blown Top Braggart

Category Barleywine
Recipe Type Extract

Fermentables

3.3 lbs. Wildflower honey
3.3 lbs. Amber malt extract
2 lbs. Wheat extract
1 lb. Light malt extract
.5 lbs. 10L crystal malt

Hops

2 oz. Northern Brewer hops (8.0%)
2 oz. Kent Goldings pellets (4.6%)
.5 oz. Kent Goldings pellets
.5 oz. Kent Goldings pellets

Other

1/4 tsp Irish Moss last 5 minutes

Yeast 1/2 teaspoon yeast energizer

Brain Death Barleywine

Category Barleywine
Recipe Type Extract

Fermentables

17-1/2 lbs. Pale dry extract
3 lbs. Crystal malt
1.5 lbs. Flaked barley
1.5 lbs. Wheat malt

Hops

68 HBUs Chinook hops (boil)
20 HBUs Cascade hops (boil)
2.5 oz. Goldings hops (finish)
10 grams Chinook hops (dry hop)

20 grams Kent Goldings hops (dry hop)
50 grams Cascade hops (dry hop)
.5 grams Herbal hops substitute

Other
 1 tsp gypsum
1 tsp Irish moss

Yeast Sierra Nevada ale yeast

Procedure This recipe makes 5 gallons of full-strength Barleywine plus 4 gallons half strength. Follow normal procedures, but brew in a 7-gallon kettle and then divide the wort into separate fermenters. The special hops substitute is a mix of hops repeatedly soaked and sparged in lukewarm water for at least 4 hours to eliminate water-soluble off-flavors. Special hops are added to the secondary fermenter about 1 week before kegging. Quantity used depends on the quality of herbs/hops.

Breakfast Barleywine

Category Barleywine
Recipe Type Extract
Delicious at bottling.

Fermentables
 14 lbs. Alexander's pale malt extract
2 oz. Black malt
1 lb. Golden brown sugar
1 lb. Honey

Hops
 2.5 oz. Hallertauer NB plugs (7.5% alpha
3--1/2 oz. Fuggles plugs (4.2% alpha

Other
 3 tsp gypsum

Yeast Vintner's Choice Champagne yeast (secondary ferment)

Procedure Primary ferment with the Belgian ale yeast, 1 week at 63F. (Very vigorous primary fermentation that took off within 12 hours).
Secondary ferment with the champagne yeast, 5 weeks at 66. Racked off trub and pitched champagne yeast. Not much activity. The Belgian must have done its trick. Still, some minor activity.

Extract Barleywine

Category Barleywine
Recipe Type Extract
With that much malt, the blow off was really! Really! REALLY! Wasteful (that is, making 4.75 gal in a 5 gal carboy.) I had to reboil and repeats the 2 gallons of foam that settled back out into nice wort.
I think 12# of syrup would have been sufficient.

Fermentables
9 lbs. Light syrup, (M&F)
6 lbs. Amber syrup

Hops
4 oz. hops to boil (Saaz, I think, but use your favorite)
2.5 oz. hops to finish (Fuggles, again, use your fave)

Yeast Wyeast European Ale yeast

Fine Line Barleywine

Category Barleywine
Recipe Type Extract

Fermentables
5.3 lbs. Edme dark SFX
1.5 lbs. Briess crystal malt (60L)

1/3 lbs. Briess chocolate malt
1/3 lbs. Briess black patent malt
.5 cup corn sugar (priming)

Hops
2 oz. Cluster pellets (90 minute boil)
1.5 oz. Northern Brewer pellets (90 minute boil)

Other solutions solutions
6 lbs. Briess Amber DMX
1 tsp dry rosemary (30 minute boil)
3 tbsp roasted chicory root (30 minute boil)

Yeast champagne yeast (secondary ferment)

Procedure I used the standard "bring specialty malts to a boil" method, and boiled only about 3 gallons of wort in my crappy ceramic coated pot which is about to become a bath chiller.

Gnarly Barleywine

Category Barleywine
Recipe Type Extract
All extract, used light, Munich, dark, lager extract
Fermentables
 6.0 Lbs. Light malt
3.0 Lbs. Munich extract
1.3 Lbs. Dark extract
1.3 Lbs. Lager extract
1.3 Lbs. Brown extract
10.0 oz. Inverted sugar
2.5 oz. Challenger hops 1 hour

Hops
 2.0 oz. Cascade hops for dry hopping

Yeast Scottish

Procedure Boil all extracts for one hour, pitch yeast, and wait for the fermentation to settle. Transfer to secondary, dry hop with 2oz cascade hops; pitch a starter of champagne yeast. Wait six months, and enjoy.

High Altitude Barleywine

Category Barleywine
Recipe Type All Grain

Fermentables
15 lb English 2-row
2 lb English crystal 53 deg

Hops
2 oz. Centennial aa=10. 2% for 60 min
3 oz. Cluster aa=7. 2% for 45 min
2 oz. American northern brewer aa=7.7% 30 min
2 oz. American northern brewer. aa=7.7% 15 min
2 oz. American northern brewer 5 min
2 oz. American northern brewer 2 min

Yeast Wyeast British ale yeast

Procedure Mash in at 115 deg f hold 30 min; add boiling water and heat to 140 deg f 30 min; add heat to 156 deg f hold until conversion is complete. Sparge with 7 gal 170 deg f water for 60 min, collect approx 8 gal wort. Boil 60 min without hops, and then boil another 60 minutes, adding hops according to the times listed above. Immersion chilling for 20 min to 72 deg f. Allow to settle for 30 min in boil pot. Split in to 2 2.5 gal batches. Add 0.7 liter Wyeast British ale starter in 1.080 wort to each 5.2 gal final volume in carboys.

Longhorn Fog Leg

Category Barleywine
Recipe Type All Grain

Fermentables
13 lb pale 2-row malt

1 lb crystal malt (40L)
4 oz. Chocolate malt
3 lb pale dry malt extract
1 lb dark brown sugar

Yeast Sierra Nevada ale yeast (Wyeast 1056)

Procedure Mash:
Mash water: 4 gallons
Mash-in: 130-121F for 30 minutes
Starch conversion: 150F for 2.5 hours
Mash-out: 170 for 5 minutes
Sparge: 4 gallons at 170F

Boil three hours total. Add extracts and hops with one hour remaining.

Primary fermentation: Kraeusen fell in 6 days.. your mileage may vary.

Secondary: Racking restarted fermentation -- next time I do this I will rack *and* splash going into secondary, since the gravity at this point was only down to 1.060. The beer stayed in secondary for about 6 weeks total.

Primed with 1/2c corn sugar.

Revenge

Category Barleywine
 Recipe Type Extract

Fermentables
12 lbs. Alexander Pale Malt
12 oz. Light Crystal Malt 8 oz. Cara-Pils Malt
7 lbs. Clover Honey (from the grocery store)

Hops
2 oz. Pride of Ringwood Hops (boil)
2 oz. Liberty Hops (finish)

Other
1 tsp. Irish Moss

Yeast Lavin 1118 Yeast (DRY)

Procedure In 1 1/2 gallons of water, add all of the grains to a hop sack and place in the brew kettle. Bring water and grains up to 165 degrees. Hold and steep for 30 minutes. Sparge grains before removing and continue to heat until wort is at a boil, at this time add the gypsum. At the boil, add the extract. After 30 minutes of boil, add boiling hops in another hop sack. Continue to boil for another 45 minutes and at this time, add the finishing hops and Irish Moss. (If you have another hop sack, place them both together in the sack and throw them on in the kettle) Let the wort boil for another 15.

Rehydrate the yeast by placing the yeast in a cup of heated water 75-90 degrees and let stand for 15 minutes.

Cool wort and add enough water to bring to a 5 gallon level in your fermentation bucket. Aerate this and pitch your yeast.

CHAPTER 2- FRUIT BEERS

Berry Strawberry

Ale Category Fruit Beers
Recipe Type Extract

Fermentables
1 lb. Crystal malt 30L
3 lbs. Amber malt syrup
3 lbs. Light malt syrup
1 lb. extra-light dry malt
5 quarts Strawberries cleaned and mashed
.75 c corn sugar

Hops
1 oz. Pride of Ringwood (boil 45min)
0.5 oz. Saaz (boil 15min)
0.5 oz. Saaz (boil 1min)

Other
1 tablespoon fruit pectin

Yeast 1 package Whitbread dry yeast

Procedure Crush grain and bring to 170degs. Remove grain and boil, etc.

After boil is completed, turn down heat and add strawberries. Try to keep wort at 160degs for 15min. Pour entire contents of pot into the primary after cooling.

Ferment in primary for 5 days. Then rack to secondary and add the fruit pectin. Let rest for three weeks. After that if you can, drop the temp. of the beer to 35degs for 1 week. If this is done, then you need to add about a teaspoon of yeast when racking to bottling pail. Let the beer rest in bottles for at least 3 weeks. The longer, the better.

Potato Beer

Category Fruit Beers
Recipe Type All Grain

Fermentables

9 lbs. Gambrinus 2-row malt
.5 lb. British Munich Malt
8 lb. Mashed potatoes
lb. Vienna Malt
lb. Rice Hulls - absolutely necessary (end of the mash)

Hops

1.5 oz. Nugget Hops 1 hr. (Mine were home grown)
1 oz. E. Kent Goldings Hops 1/2 hr.
1 oz. Wild Hops 15 min. (Substitute Tettnanger)
2 oz. Ultra Hops 5 min.
oz. Ultra Hops 1 min.
oz. E. Kent Goldings 1 min.

Other

1 tbsp. Irish moss

Yeast ale yeast

Procedure First, boil 8 lb. of well washed peeled potatoes until done. Throw out the boil water to get rid of dirt remnants and green skin flavors. Mash to a fine consistency adding water as necessary. Allow temperature to settle at 140 F. Add 2 oz. amylase enzyme and let sit as long as you have patience and care to monitor the temperature. This time affects to a great extent your conversion. It will become much thinner in consistency and sweeten. When you finally lose your patience (3 hrs for me) add the soup to the main mash and begin your protein rest for 1/2 hr. at 122 F. Raise temperature to 152 F and mash for 2 hrs. Mash out at168 F. Now you can add the Pre-rinsed rice hulls. Stir them in well, but reserve 1/2 lb. for the bottom of your lauter turn. Sparge with pH 5.7 adjusted water. Adjust pH with either lactic acid or acid blend. Boil the wort 1 1/4 hrs. Chill quickly. Divide wort into 2 carboys and allow settling for about 2 hrs. or until the cold break is well settled. Rack the wort into clean carboys, aerate well by shaking the carboys, and then pitch your yeast. Dry Munton Fison Ale yeast is excellent for this. Ferment at 68 F. When ferment is almost done, rack to secondary adding 1 tsp. of Polycarp to each carboy. Allow to settle. This unfortunately is not sufficient to clarify the potato beer. After a week rack again and add 1 packet of dissolved gelatin (do not boil your gelatin) and set the carboy in as cool a place as you can find (not freezing). When clear, rack into your Cornelius kegs and force carbonate. And/or bottle. Age 3 months for a very smooth, mellow ale with a faint mashed potato flavor. The hops are very nice too.

Pumpkin Ale

Category Fruit Beers
Recipe Type Extract

Fermentables

6 lbs. Northwestern Golden malt extract 1 lb. British crystal malt
2 lbs. Sliced up pumpkin (NOT the gross seedy junk, the stuff you crave!)

Hops

1.5 oz. Fuggles hops for 60 minutes

Other

1 tsp Allspice 1 tsp Cinnamon
1 oz. Fresh grated Ginger root
1oz fresh grated Ginger root
1 tsp Nutmeg

Yeast Wyeast #1056 (American Ale allegedly the same yeast used by SNBC)

Procedure Add all the spices (including Ginger root) for the last 10 minutes of the boil. OK, now there is some controversy over exactly WHEN to add the pumpkin: the original newsletter said to add 2 inch cubes of pumpkin to the brew-kettle 10 MINUTES before the end of the boil, and to "ferment on" the pumpkin cubes. In the batch I made for the Dixie Cup, I put the pumpkin cubes into the brew-kettle 30 minutes before the end of the boil. I'm not sure this was a good idea - I think I boiled off some pumpkin crud ("crud" is a technical term) that got into the final product. With the batch I just brewed, I am going to add mashed-up pumpkin to the secondary carboy, and rack the contents of the primary on top of it. I used this method with excellent results in a raspberry wheat beer recently. I also used a very different hopping schedule in my most recent batch: 60 minutes - 3/4 oz. Willamette (4.5% alpha) 30 minutes - 1/4 oz. Willamette 1/2 oz. Cascades (5.5% alpha) 5 minutes - 1 1/2 oz. Cascades The original recipe said to add finings to clear. I added 1 teaspoon of Irish Moss at 60, 30 and 10 minutes before the end of the boil. I am also considering finings or some other clarification agent in the secondary (pumpkin has got some CLOUDY JUNK in it!).

Pumpkin Stout

Category Fruit Beers
Recipe Type Extract

Fermentables
2 cans (29 ounces each) of Libby's 100% Pumpkin (not pumpkin pie mix)
8 oz. Flaked Barley
4 oz. Belgian Special B
6 oz. 60 L Caramel (Briess)

3 oz. Chocolate Malt
2 oz. Roasted Barley
1 3.3 pound can DMS diastatic malt extract

Hops
1 oz. Northern brewers Plugs 7.5% 60 mins
.5 oz. Styrian holdings 5.3% 30 mins
.5 oz. Hallertauer Hersbrucker 2.9% 10 mins

Other
1 cinnamon stick (2 inches or so)
.25 tsp coriander, ground
.25 tsp **cardamom**, ground
.5 tsp ginger, ground

Yeast

Procedure "Mashed" malts, pumpkin, and extract at 150 F
(65 C) for 30 mins, then sparged through grain bag. A real
mess. Final volume = ca.3 gallons Added 3.3 lbs. of Amber
Briess Extract and commenced boiling.

Yeast was Red Star Ale Yeast, rehydrated in some cooled
boiled wort. Beer was kegged/force carbonated and almost
completely gone in one evening of Christmas partying.

Canned pumpkin dissolves into a horrendously fine mush
that will settle to the bottom of your primary and cause you
to lose up to 1 gallon or more (it does not firmly settle out.)
Are the results worth it? I think so, but I will only do 2 or 3
pumpkin brews a year for the holidays, because it is messy. I
would think that using fresh, cooked pumpkin cut into 1"
cubes or so might strain out better, or they might break down
in the mash to a consistency similar to the canned stuff.
Anyone try this.

Raspberry Porter

Category Fruit Beers
Recipe Type All Grain

Fermentables
5 lbs. 2--row pale malt (mash)
1 lb. Vienna malt (mash)
.5 lbs. Munich malt (mash)
.5 lbs. 90 L. Crystal malt (mash)
.5 lbs. 20 L. Crystal malt (mash)
1 lb. Chocolate malt (steep)
.5 lbs. Cara-Pils malt (steep)
.25 lbs. Black patent malt (steep)
2.5 lbs. Australian light DME 3 lbs. Raspberries

Hops
1 oz. Chinook hops (13.7% alpha)
.75 oz. Perle hops (7.8% alpha)
1.5 oz. Cascade hops (5% alpha)

Yeast Wyeast Irish ale yeast

Procedure Mash grains using single-step infusion with 170 strike water, held at 150--160 for 1 hour. Sparge into **brew pot** where other grains were already steeped using sparging bag. Add more run off as available. Bring to boil and add DME. Boil 3/4 ounce Chinook and 1/4 ounce Perle for 60 minutes. At 30 minutes, add 1/4 ounce Chinook, 1/4 ounce Perle and 1/4 ounce Cascade. In last few minutes add 1/4 ounce Perle and 1/4 ounce Cascade. Dry hop with 1 ounce Cascade.

Quickly racked to two five gallon primaries using counter-flow chiller. Pitched Wyeast Irish Ale Yeast from DME starter into 1.054 OG wort. Racked to secondary with three pounds of raspberries (frozen) and dry hops.

Ruby Tuesday

Category Fruit Beers
Recipe Type Extract

Fermentables
7 lbs. Light malt extract syrup
7 lbs. Fresh wild raspberries
1 lbs. English crystal malt (had no lovibond rating on pkg,

Hops
2/3 oz. Cascades whole hops (~3.5% alpha)

Other
1 campden tablet
.5 cup corn sugar to prime

Yeast 1 pack Edme ale yeast (11.5g)

Procedure Brought 2--1/2 gallons water to boil with crystal malt in grain bag (removed the grain bag when water was at 170 F). Added extract and brought to boil, boiled for 60 minutes. All about hops for 45 minutes.

Chilled wort to ~100 F and strained into the carboy (prefilled with 2-- 1/2 gallons cold water). Rehydrated yeast in 90 F water for 15 minutes and pitched, topped off carboy with water, and mounted blow off tube.

After two days of healthy ferment (~75 F) added fruit. Pureed raspberries with campden tablet, added to fresh carboy (better use a 6 or 7 gallon carboy if you got it, the fruit takes up space!), purged carboy with CO2, and racked the beer into it. It swirled around a little to mix it up (don't shake it up) and put a blow off tube back on. Let sit another week and bottle. I only used 1/2 cup corn sugar to prime, and it was plenty. Didn't take a final gravity.

CHAPTER 3- LAGER

Bulwark American Lager

Category Lager
Recipe Type Extract

Fermentables
3 lbs. 5 oz. Munton & Fison American Light Malt Syrup (boil 60 mins)
1 lbs Munton & Fison Light Dried Malt Extract (boil 60 mins)
4 oz. Malto Dextrin (boil 30 mins) (note: I have no idea why I used

Hops
1 oz. Willamette Pellets (3.9% Alpha) (boil 45 mins)
.5 oz. Cascade Pellets (5.6% Alpha) (boil 5 mins)

Other
1 tsp Irish Moss (boil 10 mins)

Yeast 1.75 oz. WYeast #2035 American Lager Procedure
Brewing Log:
On commencing of boil, I added the Extracts and let boil for 15 minutes.

I added the Willamette and let boil for another 15 minutes. I added the Malto Dextrin and let boil for 20 minutes.

I added the Irish Moss and let boil for 5 minutes.

I added the Cascade and let boil for the final 5 minutes.

I transferred the wort to my 5 gallon bucket and let sit overnight. I transferred the wort from the 5 gallon bucket to my 7 gallon bucket, and aerated for 30 minutes using an aquarium pump (all equipment sanitized with bleach). I let the head settle down, pitched the yeast and let sit at room temperature. Once the yeast started showing signs of activity I moved the bucket to my garage, which was at a temperature of 54 degrees (f). After fermenting in the primary 1 week I transferred it to the secondary.

Corn Beer

Category Lager
Recipe Type All Grain

Fermentables
5 lbs. Cracked corn, sold as bird food
8 lbs. Light barley malt
.5 lb Crystal (40L.)

Hops
4 oz. Whole Hallertau

Yeast yeast from the bottom of a Saisson Dupont bottle

Procedure Mash corn at 110, for an hour, then 140 for another hour. Stir lots, since it's sticky.

Mash malted barley as usual at 110, 148, 140, and 160. I used a separate pot for the 110 1/2 hour protein rest, and then just tossed into the corn grits.

Mash water was around 26-30 quarts. Sparge to about 6 gallons after at least 3 hours in the 140-160 range.

Hops to taste, depending on what you're making. The yeast from the bottom of a Saisson Dupont bottle really does well with the corn content, but make sure you like that kind of beer first. 4 oz. whole Hallertau for 7 gallons of wort sounds about right, but hey, adjust to your tastes.

Crystal-Malt Fest

Category Lager, Amber
Recipe Type All Grain

Fermentables
10 lbs. German or Belgian pilsner malt
 6 oz. German light crystal malt (10L)
6 oz. German dark crystal malt (60L)
6 oz. English caramel malt (120L)

Hops
.75 oz. Tettnanger (4% alpha)
.75 oz. Styrian Golding (5% alpha)
.75 oz. Saaz (3% alpha)

Yeast Wyeast Munich or Bavarian lager yeast

Procedure Starch conversion rest at 150-152F for 90-120 minutes.

Ersatz Pilsner Urquell

Category Lager Pilsner
Recipe Type All Grain

Fermentables
8-1/2 pounds, 2--row pilsner malt
.5 pound, crystal malt (20 L.)
.5 pound, cara-pils malt

Hops
4 oz. Saaz Hops (60 min before end of boil)

Yeast Wyeast Bohemian lager #2124 or Munich lager #2308

Procedure Each recipe assumes 75% extract efficiency. Use the best German or Belgian pilsner malt you can find, rather than U.S. 2-row or U.S. 6-row malt. Likewise, use German or Belgian Munich malt if you can find it. In the recipes, the crystal malt and Munich malt impart some color, but otherwise will have slightly different flavoring properties.

Add hops following traditional German hop schedule: 2 ounces of Saaz 60 minutes before end of boil, 1 ounce 30 minutes before end of boil, and 1 ounce in last 10 minutes of boil. You could probably hop a bit more aggressively than indicated. You might make a final aroma addition of another 0.5-1 ounce of Saaz right before end of boil. You also might consider dry hopping.

Water should be soft.

For starch conversion, aim at 153-4 degrees F for 90 minutes.

Pilsner Urquell cold-conditions for months, so you might try an extended laagering

American Premium
Pilsner Category Lager
Recipe Type All Grain

Fermentables
6 lbs. Lager malt (I use 2-row, but 6-row is appropriate for the
1 lb Mild ale malt
1 lb Rice
.5 lb Flaked barley
.5 lb Flaked maize
4 oz. Malto-dextrin powder

Hops

.75 oz. Saaz (4.2%AA for 90min)
.25 oz. Saaz (4.2%AA for 30min) 1 oz. Cascade (4.9%AA for 2min)
1 oz. Cascade (4.9%AA for dry-hopping)

Yeast Wyeast #2112 California Lager (optional)

Procedure Boil rice for 30 minutes and add grains and water for mash --
First rest at 94F for 30 minutes to help breakdown the adjuncts --
Raise temp to 122F for 30 minutes for protein degradation --
Raise temp to 140F for 15 minutes for better head retention and clarity --
Raise temp to 153F for 45 minutes for starch conversion --
Raise temp to 158F for 20 minutes for complete conversion --
Mash out at 168F for 10 minutes -- Sparge w/168F water at < 6 pH --

Boil wort and add 3/4 oz. Saaz -- boil 60 min --
Add 1/4 oz. Saaz -- boil 30 min --
Add 1 oz. Cascade -- boil 2 min --
Force chill (if possible) -- rack to primary and aerate --
Rehydrate Nottingham yeast and pitch at 65F --
Ferment for 4-7 days or until no noticeable airlock activity --
Rack to secondary -- Drop temp to 55F --
Pitch Wyeast #2112 starter (>=400ml) at 55F --
Drop temp to 34-40F for 4-6 weeks (or until you decide to bottle) --

72 hours before bottling:
Add 1 oz. Cascade directly to secondary --
48 hours before bottling:
Add your favorite clarifier (if necessary), gelatin, Polycarp, etc. --
24 hours before bottling: Raise temp to 60F:

Bottle and let sit at 60F for 1 week, then drop temp back down for either extended laagering (34-45F) or for drinking (48-55) --

Beat Me Over the Head with a Stick

Bock

Category Lager, Bock
Recipe Type Partial Mash

Fermentables
6.6 lbs. John Bull light malt extract
3 lbs. Klages malt
.5 lbs. Chocolate malt

Hops

2--3/4 oz. 4.7% AAU Willamette flowers (60 minute boil)
.5 oz. 4.7% Willamette flowers (2 minute steep)

Other

10 grams Burton salts

Yeast lager yeast (I used MeV)

Procedure Bring 3 qt + 2 cups of water to 130 degrees. Add cracked Klages and chocolate malts (temp = 122 degrees). Rest 30 min. Add 7 cups of 200 degree water to bring temp up to 150 degrees. Rest 30 min. Bring up to 158 degrees with burner. Rest 20 minutes. Mash out at 170 degrees. Sparge with 7 quarts of 170 degree water, recycling the first runoff. Add malt extract and boil as normal. Chill the wort and pitch. Aerate vigorously with a hollow plastic tube... there's no need to get fancy equipment here. With the hollow tube I can whip up a 3" head of froth on the chilled wort. Bubbling activity is almost always evident within 8-10 hours of pitching a 12-18 oz. starter solution. Ferment as you would a lager.

Blueberry Lager

Category Lager
Recipe Type All Grain

Fermentables

4 lbs. 2-row Lager
3 lbs. Amber DME 5 lbs Cara-Pils
5 lb Crystal 40L 1 lb Honey
4 lbs. Frozen blueberries

Hops

1 oz. Tettnang - 60 mins (plugs)
1 oz. Willamette - 10 mins (plugs)
.5 oz. Saaz (finish)
.5 oz. Saaz (dry hop)

Yeast 2 packages European lager yeast (one for ferment one at bottling)

Procedure Step infusion mash, 120 for 30 minutes, 150 for 10 minutes, 158 for 15 minutes. Sparge with 1-1/2 gallons water. Boil. Add hops as indicated above. Add blueberries and finishing Saaz after cooling. Pitch yeast.

After one week, Boil 1/2 gallon water. Remove from heat. Add 3 pounds blueberries. Rack to secondary and add blueberry water mix. Add 1/2 ounce Saaz. Keep at lower temperature (lager).

George Braun

After 3 weeks, add 1-1/4 cup dry extract to 3 cups of water. Boil 20 minutes. Cool. Pour into bottling bucket and add another yeast pack. Siphon beer into the bucket.

Bohemian Pilsner

Category Lager, Pilsner
Recipe Type Extract

Hops
2.0 oz. Saaz plugs (60 minutes-bittering)
1.0 oz. Saaz plugs (30 minutes-flavor)
1.0 oz. Saaz plugs (2 minutes-aroma)
.5 oz. Saaz plugs (dry hop)

Other
3.3 lbs. Northwestern Gold ME
4.0 lbs. Alexander's Pale ME

Yeast Wyeast Bohemian Yeast directly from the pack (no starter)

Procedure I boiled the extract, 1 1/2 gallons water and hops as indicated in the recipe for one hour. Added everything by siphoning into a plastic water jug with 3 gallons cold water. Topped off with cold water. Waited for everything to drop to 65 and pitched the yeast. I let the stuff sit at around 65 for 1 day and then placed it in the back room of my basement where it sits on a nice 45 all day and night.

I racked to a secondary after 12 days (glass carboy) and dry hopped. It's been in the secondary for two days now and I took an SG reading and got 1.013. I had completely forgotten to take an OG reading, but looking at other Pilsner recipes, it seems 1.021 is a common final gravity.

Boxing Day Bock

Category Lager
Recipe Type All Grain

Fermentables
3 lb Belgian Munich Malt
10 lb Belgian Pilsener Malt
.5 lb M&F Crystal malt
2 oz. Chocolate malt

Hops
 4 oz. Hallertau plugs @ 2.9%
2 oz. Saaz plugs @ 3.1%

Yeast Wyeast Munich Lager yeast (2308)

Procedure Mix Pilsener & Munich malts in the mash tun, infuse 10.5quarts H2O@170F (mash temp 137F -- oops!), infuse additional 3qt @boiling (mash temp to 145F - -- sigh!), decoct 3qts (pretty thick) to boiling (mash temp to 156F -- finally!) Meanwhile, steep crystal in 1qt H2O @165F. Mash 1hour. Infuse 3gal @boiling to 165F, add crystal & chocolate malts & stir. 15min rest. Start sparge, recalculate 6 qts. Sparge with 6.5gal (ending sparge gravity 1.010@150F == 1.026??)
Boil 1.5 hours. Hop schedule:
2 oz. Hallertau @ 30 min
1 oz. Each Hallertau & Saaz @ 60 min
1 oz. Each @ 75 min

Chill & rack. Yield approx 4 gal @ 1.066.

Pitch yeast from 1pt starter. Move to cellar @58F. After two days, krauesen is evident, move to fridge @50F. Primary time: 6 weeks 24 hour diacetyl rest at end. Bottled at FG 1.022, laagered in the bottle.

George's April's Fool Bock

Category Lager, Bock
Recipe Type Extract

Fermentables
3.3 lb Beirkeller Dark Malt Extract
4 lb Laaglander Dutch Bock Hopped Malt Extract

Hops
0.5 oz. Tettnanger Hops (4.3%AA) --flavor, 15 minutes
0.5 oz. Tettnanger Hops aroma--added at end of boil

Yeast Wyeast 1007 German Ale Yeast

Procedure Dissolved malts in 3 gallons of warm water. Boiled for 30 mins. Added flavor hops and boiled an additional 15 minutes. Removed from heat and stirred in aroma hops. Ice bathed for 20 minutes to 90*F. Added to *new* carboy (which I have nicknamed "Bertha") that had 2.5 gallons of cold tap water. Added more tap water to yield 5 gallons. Shook the hell out of the carboy (no I did not roll around the floor this time). Shook some more.

Pitched yeast and shook some more. Popped an airlock onto the carboy and went to bed at 1:00 AM. This morning I am happy to report I have a krausen starting.

Hefe-Hafer Ale (2.5 Gallons)

Category German Ale
Recipe Type All Grain

Fermentables
1500.0 Grams Briess Pale 2-Row Malt
1500.0 Grams Rolled Brewers Oatmeal

Hops
7.0 Grams German Hallertau Mitt
1.0 Grams German Hallertau Mitt (dry hop)

Yeast Wyeast 3068 Weihenstephan

Procedure Mashing Procedure: Acid Rest - 99degF - 30min Protein Rest - 120degF - 30min Protein Rest - 130degF - 30min Conversion - 160degF - 30min No Mash Out Sparge - 160degF - 30min Wort flow benefits from adding 1cup Rice Hulls to mash just prior to sparging Boiling Procedure: I don't like the flavor Irish moss adds to beer so I don't use it, but the finished beer is definitely clearer if you do use it. Heavy boil - 30min Heavy boil - 45min (7g hop added at beginning of second boil) Rest (no heat) - 30min Cool as quickly you possibly can. I use a home built refrigeration system that cools the wort to roughly 50degF faster than I can gravity drain. Pitch yeast and allow fermentation to begin before adding 1g hop for dry hopping. Primary fermentation is usually complete within 7 days. Transfer to secondary fermenter for 7 more days. Rack to bottles priming for roughly 2.5-2.6Vol store for about 30 to 160days. The oats contribute a large amount of fat to the final product. Waiting longer than 160 days to drink the final product begins to decline. Wort flow benefits from adding 1cup Rice Hulls to mash just prior to sparging.

Hurricane Helles

Category Lager
Recipe Type All Grain
Here's a nice Munich Helles lager recipe I've been using for the last year or so - makes a very drinkable beer. It's based on a recipe in Miller's

Fermentables
7 lb two-row lager malt

1 lb Vienna malt
Hops

6-8 HBU Tettnang, 1 addition at 45 minutes

Yeast Wyeast 2308 Munich Lager from 1/2 gallon starter

Procedure Mash schedule: 30 minutes @ 122F, 30 minutes @ 140F, 30-60 minutes @ 155F, 10 minutes @ 165F, sparge 5 gallons @ 168F.
Chill to 48F and pitch yeast. Ferment 2 weeks @ 48F, rack to secondary and let the temperature rise to mid 50's for diacetyl rest for 2-3 days. Then back to 32F for lagering 4-6 weeks.

Kentucky Sour Mash Beer

Category Sour Mash
Recipe Type All Grain

Fermentables
8.5 lbs American 2 row malt
1.5 lb Rye malt
1 lb Cara Pils malt
1 lb 120L Crystal malt
.25 oz. Black Patent malt - finely crushed

Hops
1 oz. Galena hops (60 min) AA=11.5%
.5 oz. Cascade hops (30 min) AA=4.6%
.5 oz. Cascade hops (15 min) AA=4.6%
.5 oz. Fuggles hops (2 min)

Other

2 tsp Gypsum per 5 gal RO water
.5 tsp Epsom salts per 5 gal RO water

.25 tsp table salt per 5 gal RO water
.25 tsp powdered Irish moss (10 min)

Yeast Yeast Labs American Ale yeast

Procedure Add 2 lb of 2 row malt to 0.5 gal 130F water
Mash malts 30 min @ 122F
Add 1 pt boiling water
Mash malt 30 min @ 140F
Add 1 pt boiling water
Mash malt 30 min @ 158F
Mashout @ 175F for 5 minutes
Cool to 90F and stir in yogurt culture
Sour for 2 1/2 days
Add remaining malt to 2.5 gal 130F water
Mash malts 30 min @ 122F
Add 3 qt boiling water
Mash malts 30 min @ 140F
Add 3 qt boiling water
Mash malts 30 min @ 158F to conversion
Add Black Patent malt
Mashout at 175F for 5 minutes
Combine mashes
Sparge at 170F
Boil for 75 min Cool and pitch yeast

Maerzen Beer

Category Lager, Amber
Recipe Type Partial Mash

Fermentables
4 lbs. Pale malt
3 lbs. Light dry extract
.5 lbs. Crystal malt (40L)
2 oz. Chocolate malt
.5 lbs. Toasted malt
.5 lbs. Munich malt

2 oz. dextrin malt

Hops
2.5 oz. Tettnanger hops (4.2 alpha)
. 5 oz. Cascade hops (5.0 alpha)

Other
3 tsp gypsum

Yeast Vierka dry lager yeast

Procedure Make up yeast starter 2 days before brewing.
Grind all grains together, dough-in with 5 cups warm water.
Use 3 quarts water at 130 degrees to bring up to protein rest
temperature of 122 degrees. Set for 30 minutes. Add 8 pints
of boiling water and heat to 154 degrees. Set for at least 30
minutes. Bring to 170 degrees for 5 minutes for mash out.
Sparge with 2 gallons water. Add dry extract, bring to boil.
Boil 15 minutes and add one ounce of Tettnanger. Boil one
hour. Add 1 ounce of Tettnanger at 30 minutes. Add 1/2
ounce of Tettnanger and 1/2 ounce of Cascade at 5 minutes
(with Irish moss if desired). Strain and chill. Rack off trub.
Pitch yeast.
Ferment at 68 degrees for 3 days. Rack to secondary and
lager 18 days at 42 degrees. After 18 days keg and lager an
additional 17 days.

Nightingale Dopple Bock
Category Lager, Bock
Recipe Type Extract

Fermentables
7 lbs. Light Scottish Malt Extract 1 lb. Dry Dark Malt Extract
1.5 lbs. 80L Crystal Malt 6 oz. Chocolate Malt   2 oz. Black
Patent Malt 8 oz. Dextrin Malt
2/3 cup corn sugar for priming

Hops
2 oz. Perle Hops (bittering) alpha=7. 6%
1 oz. Hallertauer Hops (aromatic) alpha=3. 9%

Other
.25 tsp brewing salts
.5 tsp Gypsum

Yeast 2 packets of Red Star Lager yeast

Procedure Mash crushed crystal and dextrin malts in a pan of water at 150F for 1 hour. Strain through colander into the main kettle and sparge with 150F water until it runs clear. Add enough water to kettle to dissolve extracts (approx. 3 gallons). Dissolve extracts, salt and gypsum into kettle and bring to a ROLLING boil. Stir in 1/2 oz. Perle hops and boil 15 min. Stir in 1 oz. Perle Hops and boil 15 min. Stir in chocolate and black patent malts (UNCRUSHED!) and boil 15 min. Stir in 1/2 oz. Perle hops and boil 15 min. Add Hallertauer hops in the last minute of the boil. Strain through a nylon meshed colander into Primary fermentor. Top up to 5 gallons with cold water. Cool wort as fast as possible. (I cooled it to 80 degrees in 9 minutes.) At 80F add yeast. Ferment for 12 days at 40-48 degrees. Rack it into the secondary and let it sit and ferment VERY slowly for 1 month at 32-40 degrees. Bottle and let age for a full month at 34 degrees.

Surprised Frog

Lager Category Lager, Pale
Recipe Type Extract

Fermentables
3.3 lbs. Munton & Fison extra light extract
~0.4 lbs. (2/5 pound), Briess amber extract
.5 lbs. Crystal malt (40 L.)
12 oz. Clover honey
.5 cup corn sugar

Hops

1 oz. Cascade hop pellets (60 minute boil)

Other

3 oz. Grated ginger root (15 minute boil) 1/3 licorice stick

Yeast Wyeast Pilsen liquid yeast

Procedure I measured the OG at 1026, although in hindsight I think the brew was still a little warm. . . . Let's call it 1035 or so. I put this in my fridge (42 F) on 9 December; in hopes that it would be finished by the time I got back from Xmas break. It certainly wasn't! On 16 January I measured the specific gravity at 1021, and it was still pretty sweet. On 8 February, though I knew that it was not done fermenting, I bottled with 1/2 cup corn sugar and put all the bottles back in my fridge. A day later, I decided to move two bottles into my pantry, to see if anything interesting would happen. ..

Swill Clone

Category Lager
Recipe Type Extract

Fermentables
3 cups 20LV is crystal malt
3.3 lbs. John Bull dark unshipped extract syrup
3.5 cups Munton and Fison unhopped plain amber dry malt
extract (20 EBC ish)

Hops
1 oz. Kent Goldings hop pellets (boiling)
.5 oz. Cascade hop pellets (finishing)

Other
.5 tsp Burton water salts (if needed)
.5 tsp gypsum (if needed)
.5 tsp Irish Moss

Yeast Lager Yeast (please use something good!)

Procedure Well, here goes... keep it simple and fun! Before
you start... why not get your yeast starter going?

Crack the crystal in a blender or whatever you like to crack
with (don't bowdlerize it!) bring it to a boil with one gallon of
cold water. At the first sign of a boil, strain the liquid into
your normal boiling pot (don't squeeze, smash, or squish the
grain... just let the wort run out).

Add one gallon (or two if the pot is large enough) of water,
the water, salts, and extracts to the pot and bring to a boil.
Boil for fifteen minutes, then add the boiling hops and
continue boiling for 30 minutes (keep on stirring, but try to
keep the pot covered as much as possible).

Add the Irish moss, stir for one minute.

Add the finishing hops. Stir and cover for three minutes.

Place (chill first if you like) in the fermenter and top to 5.5 gallons. Pitch when cool (as if you didn't know this part). I normally use a two stage system. I'll rack it once after the head falls. When the bubbler parts 2 or less times per minute, I'll bottle or keg. If you are bottling, I would suggest using somewhere between 1/2 and 3/4 cup corn sugar, or 1/2 cup of honey for priming... I hope I didn't forget anything...

Note: If you serve this beer to newbie's or wimps, serve it COLD!

Samuel Adams Taste-Alike Beer

Category Lager
Recipe Type Extract

Fermentables
1 can Munton & Fison Premium Kit
2 1 1 lb. Packages Amber DME
1 cup corn sugar (for priming)

Hops

1 1 1 oz. Package Hallertauer hop pellets
1 1 1 oz. Package Tettnang hop pellets

Yeast 1 Packet yeast (under cap)

Procedure Remove label from Kit and stand in warm water for 15- 20 minutes. In a pot sufficient to boil 2 gallons of liquid, empty DME. Open can of malt and empty contents into pot onto DME. Using one gallon hot water, rinse out can and add to pot. Turn on heat and carefully bring to a boil. Ass package of Hallertauer hops, Adjust heat and simmer for 20 minutes. Add Tettnang hops and simmer for 10 minutes. Meanwhile, put 4 gallons cold water into primary fermenter. When boil is complete, the empty hot wort into cold water. When temperature reaches 80 degrees Fahrenheit, open yeast and sprinkle onto surface of the wort and cover tightly.

Place fermentation lock with water in lid. Allow the beer to ferment for four days in primary fermenter,

Transfer to clean secondary fermenter and allow to ferment for an additional ten to fourteen days.

Syphon beer from secondary fermenter into the clean bottling bucket. Dissolve priming sugar in a small amount of beer and add to bottling bucket. Fill clean bottles and cap. Let stand for five days at room temperature and then move to a cool place.

Beer will be carbonated in three weeks and will improve for several months

Sierra Nevada Helles Bock

Category Lager
Recipe Type All Grain

Fermentables
10 lb lb British Pale Ale Malt
0.5 lb by British Crystal Malt (50 L)

Hops
1 oz. oz Perle (8.1%)
.5 oz. Cascade Whole Hops - Flavor
1 oz. Cascade Whole Hops - To Be Dry Hopped Next Week

Yeast 500 ml Starter of WYeast 1056

Procedure Mashed the pale ale malt and crystal in 13 quarts treated (i.e. boiled) water at 150 F for 1.5 hours in a 10 gal Gott with a Phils Phalse Bottom.

Sparged with 4+ gal acidified (1/8 tsp "acid blend") to pH = 5.5 water at 170 F. Sparged to 6.5 gal. The gravity at 6.5 gal was 1053. This implies:

(53 pts) X (6.5gal) / 10.5 lbs. = 32.8 pts/lb/gal!
When boiled to 5.5 gal and racked to primary that yields an OG of
62.6. What should I call this stuff? Sierra Nevada Potent Ale?

Anyway, the mash went very well. The temperature drop was only two degrees over the 1.5 hrs (I preheated the Gott). Now sparging, that is another story. I was somewhat overwhelmed by the sparging: I kept drawing off the wort and recalculating it, but it never seemed to clear the way I expected it. I finally said to hell with it and ran off the initial wort and proceeded to sparge with water to 6.5 gal. There was still good sugar in the sparge at this point.

Your Father's Mustache

Category Lager
Recipe Type Partial Mash

Fermentables
7 lbs. American six row malt (80%)
1.75 lbs. Flaked maize (20%)

Hops
25 g. Cluster hops pellets @7. 5% - 1hr boil
.25 oz. Styrian Goldings @5.2% - 10 min. boil plus
.25 oz. Styrian Goldings @5.2% - 15 min. settling

Other
9 gallons moderately (temp.) hard well water boiled to soften

Yeast New Ulm yeast Procedure Mash schedule:
Doughed in 8.5 qts.58C water to get -->
50C protein rest, 30 min., (pH 5.5), then infused w/ 3 qts.
boiling water to -->
60C sac. rest for 15 minutes, then boosted w/ burner to -->
70C sac. rest for 40 minutes, then boosted w/ burner to -->
76C mash off for 10 min.
Lautered in insulated Zapap, collected 7 gal. @ 1.041 for 32.8
p/p/g. Note - Beautifully clear wort with minimum
recirculation, easy sparge. This six-row is beautiful to work
with.

Boil - 1 hour, beautiful hot break, like egg drop soup

Hopped to 25 IBU target.

Counter current cooled to 64F, 4.75 gallons collected in 1.055,
then diluted to 5.5 gallons at 1.048 in 7 gallon carboy, force
chilled in snowbank to 50F. Pitched New Ulm yeast from
bottom of 3 liter starter. Fermented @ 50F - 52F 12 days,
racked, lagered seven weeks @ 33F, kegged, conditioned with
10 psi @ 38F, then dispensed at 42F-44F. The flavor showed
best at mid 40sF and when drawn to give a good head and
reduced carbonation. (Most beer shows best like this).

CHAPTER 4- PALE ALE

Alex's Delicious E.S.B.

Category Pale Ale
Recipe Type Extract

Fermentables
6 lbs. Munton's amber dry malt extract
1 lb 60l crystal
4 oz. British chocolate malt (for a smoother, less burned flavor)

Hops
1 oz.5.3 alpha East Kent Goldings 60 minutes
0.5 oz. 4.5 alpha Fuggles 30 minutes
0.5 oz.5.0 alpha tetnanger 10 minutes
1 oz. 3.5 alpha Saaz 5 minutes
1 oz. 3.5 alpha Saaz dry hop in secondary

Other
2 tbsp of gypsum
.5 tsp Irish Moss fifteen minutes before end of boil
.5 cup corn sugar to prime

Yeast wyeast London Ale Yeast

Procedure Put grains in 1.5 gal of water and bring to a boil. Remove grains, take pot off heat, and add gypsum and malt extract. Stir well until the extract is thoroughly dissolved. Put back on heat and bring to boil. Add Goldings. Wait thirty minutes and add Fuggles. Wait fifteen minutes and add Irish moss. Wait another five minutes and add tetnanger. Wait five minutes more and add Saaz. Cool when the hour is up and sparge into fermenter. Pitch yeast. Rack after four days and dry hop for three weeks in secondary.

This beer should be fermented between sixty five and seventy degrees. You want some esters in an ESB for complexity. The chocolate malt will give the beer a roasted taste in the background. I do not call this an English ESB because of the German and Czech hops used for flavoring and aroma, but it's every bit as tasty.

Al's Pale Ale

Category Pale Ale
Recipe Type Extract

Fermentables
3 lbs. Laaglander light dry malt extract
.5 lbs. Crushed crystal malt (40 L.)
5--1/2 oz. Laaglander light, dry extract (priming)

Hops
1 oz. Cluster pellets (60 minute boil)
.5 oz. Fuggles pellets (15 minute boil)
1 oz. Goldings, Fuggles, Cascade, or Willamette whole hops

Other
1/3 oz. Burton water salts
5--1/2 Gal water

Yeast Wyeast #1028 "London Ale" yeast

Procedure Steep the crushed crystal malt in a grain bag in the water as you bring it from cold to 170F, then remove. Don't boil the grains! I use two polyester hop bags, one for each addition, to simplify removing the hops after the boil. The wort must be cooled to 70 or 80F before aeration. I use an immersion chiller, which brings it from 212F to 70F in 15 minutes, and then pour the beer through a large funnel into the fermenter on top of the yeast. I recommend the blow off method of fermentation---non-blow off versions of this beer have tasted harsh, astringent and too bitter.

Primary fermentation: 3 weeks in glass at 66F. Dry hops added directly into the fermenter (no hop bag) over kraeusen falls (about 4-6 days). No secondary. Boil the priming extract in 16 ounces of water for 15 minutes to sanitize.

Al's Special London Ale

Category Pale Ale
Recipe Type Extract

Fermentables
6.6 lbs. M&F unhopped light malt extract
1 lb. Laaglander light dried malt extract
1 lb. Crushed 2-row British crystal malt ~40L

Hops
2 oz. Northern Brewer Pellets (6.2%AA) (60 min. boil)
.5 oz. East Kent Goldings (whole) (5 minute boil)
1 oz. East Kent Goldings (whole) (dry hop last 7 days before

Other
.5 tsp Burton water salts
.25 tsp Irish Moss (15 minutes)
.5 cup corn sugar for priming

Yeast 8 ounce starter of Wyeast #1028

Procedure Start with 5--1/2 gallons tap water. Steeped crushed crystal malt in a grain bag while the liquor and Burton water, salts went from tap water temperature up to 165F. Remove grain bag and let the wort drain out of it. After boiling down to 5 gallons, OG was 1071, so I added an additional 1/2 gallon of boiled water (not a big deal, but hop utilization would have been different with a 6 gallon boil). By the way, Chicago water is quite soft---I suspect distilled would be close enough.

Fermentation in glass will blow off, at 68F. Dry hops simply stuffed into the primary after fermentation ended, seven days before bottling.

Heiko's Ale

Category German Ale
Recipe Type All Grain

Fermentables
8 lbs. Belgian 2-row Pilsen (1.5L)
2 lbs. Belgian 2-row Munich (~4L)
.5 lb. Belgian 2-row Aromatic (~21L)
.5 lb. Belgian 2-row Carapils (?L)
.5 lb. Belgian 2-row Caramunich (~64L)
0.75 oz. Crystal " 30 min.

Hops
3.25 oz. Crystal (pellets, 3.3%) 60 min.

Other
.5 lb. German wheat (?L)

Yeast 1007 German Ale yeast

Procedure I mashed (single infusion) at 152F for 1.5 hours. Primary fermented at around 55-60F for 6 days. I split the batch after the primary - put 1 gallon in my fridge at around 38F for two weeks, while the other 4 gallons sat in a carboy in my basement at around 70F. The beer was very spicy (from the 1007?) at first, but mellowed out nicely after about 4 weeks. The cold-conditioned gallon was smoother, and more drinkable at an earlier age (~2 weeks after bottling) than the warm-conditioned portion. The cold-conditioned beers were also *brilliantly clear* It was perfectly balanced (to me), with a complex maltiness that I haven't had in any of my past beers. The IBU's were around 36, using Tinseth's calculator.

The color was perfect (dark copper?), though the alcohol was probably a bit on the high side for the style.

America Discovers Columbus

Category Pale Ale
Recipe Type All Grain

Fermentables
11 lb Schreier 2-row pale malt
1 lb DWC Munich
0.6 lb DWC CaraVienne
0.5 lb DWC Biscuit
0.5 lb Gambrinus Honey Malt
0.25 lb DWC carapils

Hops
1.5 oz. Columbus hop pellets (12.5% alpha, 60 minute boil)
.5 oz. Columbus hops (15 minute boil)
.25 oz. Cascade hops (4.1% alpha, 15 minute boil)
.5 oz. Columbus (dry hop one week in primary)

Other
.5 oz. Columbus (finish)

Yeast ale yeast (Wyeast 1272 or 1056---see notes)
Procedure Mashed at 157-155F for 65 min. Water -
essentially deionize with = tsp gypsum
I split a 5 gallon batch into two glass fermenters. Wyeast
1272 was pitched into the first 2 gallons siphoned out of the
kettle and Wyeast 1056 got the last 2.5 gallons with a little
more trub. Both yeasts were pitched from 3 cup starters.

Amber Ale

Category Amber Ale
Recipe Type All Grain

Fermentables
10 lbs. American 2-row pale malt
1 lb Vienna Malt

.5 lb Cara-pils malt
1 lb light Crystal malt
.5 lb crystal malt (60L)
.5 cup chocolate malt

Hops
1 oz. Cascade hops (boil)
.5 oz. Fuggles hops (flavor)
.5 oz. Cascade hops (finishing)

Yeast 1000 ml Yeast starter- Wyeast Chico Ale

Procedure Mash grains in 4.3 gallons of water at 75 deg C, to bring temp to 67 deg C. Hols at 64-67degC for 1 hour and 20 minutes. Sparge with 4 gallons of 77 deg C water. (Mash pH was between 5.0 and 5.5). Collect wort, boil for one hour etc. Chill with wort chiller. Pour into fermenter, allowing pelletized hops and cold break to settle for a few hours. Rack wort to another clean fermenter. Aerate, pitch yeast.

Bass Clone

Category Pale Ale
Recipe Type Extract

Fermentables
6.6 lbs. Munton & Fisons light unhopped liquid malt extract
1.5 lb Crystal Malt 20L
1.25 cup Light DME or 3/4 cup corn sugar (priming)

Hops
1 oz. Kent Goldings hops 5.0 AA (boil)
.5 oz. Fuggle hops 4.8 AA (boil)
.5 oz. Willamette hops (finish)

Other

2.5 Gal Artesian bottled water or boil and cool water, store in sanitized
1 tsp Gypsum 1/2 tsp. Irish Moss

Yeast 1 pkg. #1098 British Ale Liquid Yeast

Procedure Add crushed grains to 2 1/2 gallons of cold tap water, add gypsum. Heat to 170 degrees, remove from heat, cover and let sit for 15 minutes. Remove grains from liquid, add liquid malt extracts and boiling hops. Boil for 60 minutes. Add Irish moss in last 15 minutes of boil. Add finishing hops last 2 minutes of boil. After boiling, cover pot and set into cold water bath in sink for 30 minutes. Add 2 1/2 gallons of cold water to the 5 gallon carboy. Add cooled wort to carboy. Shake carboy to add oxygen to wort. Add yeast packet., shake carboy again to mix yeast.

Beginner's Luck Brown Ale

Category Brown Ale
Recipe Type Extract

Fermentables

4 lb malt extract syrup 6 oz. Crystal malt
1.5 oz. Black malt   2 oz. Roasted barley
1 oz. Flaked or rolled barley 1 oz. Wheat malt
28 oz. Dark brown sugar

Hops
2 oz. Northern Brewer hops 1 oz. Goldings hops

Other
2 oz. Lactose

Yeast ale yeast

Procedure Hops: these are two of the six or so types available here in the UK; I'm afraid I don't know what the US equivalents would be because I've been brewing only since my transplantation from the States in early '92. [If anyone knows a reasonable set of hops equivalences, I'm all ears.] Northern Brewer is a very sharp hop that is a prime-requisite for British dark beers and stouts (and some pale ales); Goldings is a much "rounder" hope that is a prominent component of southern-English bitters. US brewers use your best guesses, I guess. Procedure: I treat my water with 0.25 tsp salt per gallon to adjust pH; the water here (Bristol, in the SW) is fairly soft by UK standards but contains some dissolved $CaCO3$. I have had no difficulties whatever using tap water. I dissolve the malt extract and then boil the adjunct grains + hops in it for about an hour. I then strain a couple of kettlefuls (kettlefuls?) of hot water into the primary through the spent grains and hops to rinse them. I dissolve the sugar in a couple of pints of warm water and add this to the wort, then top up with cold water to 5 gallons. When the wort is cool, I then measure OG (usually about 1035 to 1039), then add the lactose and pitch the (top-fermenting) yeast. The lactose gives just a hint of residual sweetness in the final brew; if that's not to your taste, omit it. This brew ferments to the quarter-gravity stage in about 3 days when temperatures are about 20C (70F) and in about 5 days when temps are about 10C (mid-40s F). Final gravity is usually about 1005, resulting in ABV's in 4.5 to 5%. I prime my secondary fermentation vessel with about 1 tsp of dark brown sugar, and usually let it sit in the secondary 7 to 10 days, adding finings after the first 48 hours or so. I have not tried dry-hopping this recipe. I prime my bottles with 1/2 tsp of brewer's glucose; maturation is sufficiently complete in about 10 days, but obviously the longer the better

Belgian Ale

Category Belgian Ale
Recipe Type All Grain

Fermentables
8.5 lbs. 2-row pale malt
1.5 lbs. Munich Malt
4 oz. Crystal Malt (35 Lovibond)
1 oz. Chocolate Malt
1 lb. Demerrara sugar

Hops
1 oz. Hallertau (3.8%)
.75 oz. Stryian Goldings(5.0%)
.5 oz. Saaz (3.5%)

Other
.5 tsp Gypsum Mash & Sparge each
1 Tsp Irish Moss

Yeast Chimay Yeast starter (1.5 Qts.)

Procedure Mash in with 12 qts. water @ 122 degrees F. and rest 30 min. Raise to 140 F and rest 10-15 min. Raise to 150 F and wait till starch is converted(90 min.) Mash out at 168 F and rest 10 min. Sparge with 168 F water to collect 23-24 liters (5.75-6.0 Gallons) Boil for 70-90 min. with the following hop schedule -- 1 oz. Hallertau for 65-70 min. 1/2 oz. Stryian Goldings for 65 min.-- 1/4 oz. S. Goldings for 40 min. 1/2 oz. Saaz for the final 3 min. -- Cool to pitching temperature(68-70F) and pitch yeast starter. I racked this brew when primary fermentation was done and added 1/4 oz. of Saaz to the secondary (dry hop) and let sit for 2 weeks before bottling. Added 3/4 cup of dextrose to prime. Make sure you let this beer condition in the bottle for at least 3 months before sampling. Actually it gets better after 6 months in the bottle. By the way, this recipe is for 5 U.S. gallons and you may want to increase or decrease the amount of grains depending on the efficiency of your system. My starting gravity was 1.068 and finished off at 1.012.(about 7.4% A/V).

Belgian Dubbel

Category Belgian Ale
Recipe Type All Grain

Fermentables
9.5 lbs. Pale malt
4 oz. Crystal malt (20 deg L)
4 oz. Brown malt
.75 lbs. Sugar
3 oz. Priming sugar or 2-2.5 volumes of CO_2

Hops
1 oz. Styrian (5% alpha) (bittering)
.3 oz. Hallertauer (bittering)
.3 oz. Saaz (aroma)

Yeast trappist ale yeast starter

Procedure Soft water is recommended with a mash temperature (single infusion) of 150-152 Deg F.

Bob's Sandia Pale Ale

Category Pale Ale
Recipe Type Extract

Fermentables
6 lbs. Light dry malt extract 1 lb carapils malt
.25 cup malto dextrine

Hops
1 oz. Northern brewer's pellets (boil)

2 oz. Cascade plugs (aroma and dry hop)

Yeast 2/3 cup dextrose and small amount of any brewer's yeast for prime and bottle

Procedure Start Wyeast in the usual fashion (at least 24 hrs prior). Steep grains at 158F for 15min in 1 gallon water, sparge with 1 gallon ~170F. Start boil with this original 2 gallons add DME, Malta dextrine, and northern brewers pellets, boil 45 min, add 1/2 oz. Cascade, boil 10 more minutes, then add another 1/2 oz. cascade and turn off heat. Let sit 5 minutes, cool and add to ~3.5 gallons for a total volume 5 - 5.5 gallons. Pitch yeast (should be ~ 1 liter of starter).

Note this yeast (Wyeast 1968) activity is low and very little carbon dioxide is given off. This yeast is very flocculants and it will leave bottled beer flat, so just add a small amount of any other yeast with the dextrose at bottling to get good carbonation, however it produces a very smooth character to the brew that makes it worth using.

Primary fermentation is complete in 4 days. Rack to secondary and add 1/2 cascade (dry hop). Bottle after ~ 7 days in secondary using 2/3 cup dextrose, and being careful to add additional yeast a 1/4 tsp of any dry yeast is plenty.

Brewhaus I.P.A.

Category Pale Ale
Recipe Type All Grain

This beer is best when consumed young. It will acquire a drier character as it ages.

Fermentables
11 lbs. 2-Row Klages Malt
1 lb. Crystal malt (40 Lovibond)

.5 lbs. Toasted malt (see below)

Hops

2 oz. Northern Brewer hops (7.1% alpha - boil)
1 oz. Cascade hops (6.0% alpha - finish)
.25 oz. Fuggle or Styrian Golding hop pellets (dry hop)

Other
.5 tsp gypsum (to harden water)
Lactic Acid (enough to bring mash water to pH 5.2) 1 oz. Oak Chips (optional)
1 tsp gelatin finings 1 tsp Irish Moss

Yeast Ale yeast

Procedure Toasted Malt: Spread 2-row Klages on cookie sheet and toast at 350 degrees until reddish brown in color. Mash grain in 12 quarts mash water (treated with gypsum and lactic acid) at 154 degrees until conversion is complete. Sparge with 170 degree water to collect 6 gallons. Bring wort to boil and boil for 15 minutes before adding hops. Add 1/2 of boiling hops. Boil for 30 minutes and add remaining boiling hops. Boil for another 45 minutes and add Irish moss. Boil for a final 30 minutes. The total boiling time is 2 hours. Cut heat, add aromatic hops, and let rest for 15 minutes, or until trub has settled. Force cool wort to yeast pitching temperature. Transfer to primary fermenter and pitch yeast. Add dry hops at end of primary fermentation. Transfer to clean, sterile carboy when fermentation is complete. Boil oak chips for one minute to sterilize and add chips and gelatin to carboy. Age until desired oak flavor is achieved. Allow bottled beer to age two weeks before consuming.

Carp Ale

Category Pale Ale
Recipe Type Extract

Fermentables
 3 lbs. Munton & Fison light DME
 3 lbs. M&F amber DME
 1 lbs. Crystal malt

Hops
 2.6 oz. Fuggles hops (4.7% alpha= 12.22 AAU)
 1 oz. Kent Goldings hops (5.9% alpha = 5.9 AAU)

Other
 1/4 tsp Irish moss

Yeast 1 pack Brewer's Choice #1098 (British ale yeast)

Procedure Break seal of yeast ahead of time and prepare a starter solution about 10 hours before brewing.
Bring 2 gallons water to boil with crushed crystal malt. Remove crystal when boil starts. Fill to 6 gallons and add DME. After boiling 10 minutes, add Fuggles. At 55 minutes, add a pinch of Irish moss. At 58 minutes, add Kent Goldings. Cool (I used an immersion chiller) to about 80 degrees. Pitch yeast and ferment for about a week. Rack to secondary for 5 days. Keg.

Dana's Smilin' Irish Eyes Red Ale
Category Pale Ale
Recipe Type Extract

Fermentables
 6 lbs. Alexander's Pale Malt Extract Syrup
 1 lb. Orange Blossom Honey
 1 lb. (4 cups) Belgian Special B (200 L)

Hops
 3 oz. Cascade Hop Pellets

Other
1 tsp Irish moss

Yeast 1 pack Wyeast #1084 Irish Ale

Procedure Place cracked grains in 2 quarts cold water and bring temperature up to 170 degrees. Steep for 15 minutes and sparge into **brew pot**. Add malt extract and 1 oz. hops and boil for 45 minutes. Add Irish moss, 1 oz. hops, and honey & boil for 15 more minutes. Remove from heat & add remaining 1 oz. hops. Cool quickly, add to 3 gallons cold water in primary fermenter, and pitch yeast. Rack to secondary after vigorous fermentation subsides. Bottle when fermentation completes.

Dean's Pirahana

Category Pale Ale
Recipe Type Extract

Fermentables
0.5 Lbs. Breiss Cara Pils
0.5 Lbs. Briess Crystal 40L
0.5 Lbs. Weyer Lt. Munich
8.0 Lbs. Light malt extract (liquid)

Hops
1.0 oz. Chinook (12.2 aa) 60 min
0.5 oz. Cascade (4.9aa) @ 30 min
0.5 oz. Cascade (4.9aa) @10 min
0.5 oz. Cascade (4.9aa) at flameout steep 5-10 min
1.5 oz. Cascade (4.9aa) dry hopped in secondary

Yeast Whites Labs California Ale. WLP001

Procedure Bring water to 160 degrees f, add grains (preferably in a grain bag) to the water and turn the fire off. cover and steep for 30 min. Remove grain bag and hold it above the pot in a strainer or colander and sparge it with a quart of 170 degree water. Bring water to a boil. Turn off the heat (to prevent scorching) and add the malt extract mixing until fully dissolved. Turn heat back on and bring to a rolling boil. Add hops according to schedule above. Cool wort and add cold water and wort to make 5 gallons in primary fermenter. Pitch yeast @ 70-75 degrees f. Ferment one week and rack to secondary fermenter and 1.5 ounces of cascades. (dry hopping). After one week more beer is ready to bottle. Using 3/4 cup of corn sugar for priming.

Dragon's Rest Ale

Category Pale Ale
Recipe Type Extract

Fermentables

3 Lbs. Laaglander Amber DME
3 Lbs. Laaglander Light DME
2 Lbs. 100% Pure Barley Malt Syrup

Hops

3 Oz. Fuggles Hops 4.1% Alpha (boiling)
1 Oz. Kent-Golding Hops 5.0% Alpha (finishing)

Other

4 Tbsp. Ground Cardamom
1 tsp. Irish Moss

Yeast 1 Pkg. Wyeast #1028 London Ale (in starter of 3 cups water 1 cup dry extract)

Procedure Prepare yeast according to package. Then make a starter from ingredients listed boil 10 mins. Sanitize a Qt. beer bottle and pour starter into bottle. Cool to pitching temperature and add yeast from pkg. Fit with fermentation lock. Ferment. Be ready to pitch into wort by high krausen (foaminess) (18-24 hrs)
Add extracts and barley syrup to 1 gallon cold water. Bring to boil. Add boiling hops and 3 Tbsp. of the Cardamom, boil one hour. 10 minutes to end of boil add 1/2 oz. of the finishing hops, Irish moss and the rest of the cardamom. 3 minutes to end of boil add 1/2 oz. of the finishing hops. Sparge through cheesecloth into 4 gallons very cold water in primary fermenter. Cool and pitch starter. Agitate wort well (stirs)

Boil primer ingredients 10 minutes. Cool. Add to beer and bottle.

Easy, Delicious Old Ale

Category Strong Ale
Recipe Type Extract

Fermentables

1 lb. British/English 2-row
1 lb. 37-64L crystal
8 lbs. Alexander's Pale DMS (or equivalent)
2/3 cup chocolate malt
1/3 cup blackstrap molasses (mom)
1/2# clover honey (optional)

Hops

2 oz. Kent Golding (60 minute boil)
2 oz. Fuggles (15 minutes)
1 oz. Hallertau - 5 minutes (aroma)
1 oz. Hallertau - steep for 3 minutes with heat off (aroma)

Other

Gypsum as needed
Irish Moss at final 15 minutes

Yeast WYeast London Ale yeast or Williams Brewing Triple Ale liquid yeast pack

Procedure Mash grains at 148-158 degrees for 1 hour. Also works well with simple "steep in water until just before water boils method." I do a "quickie" sparge with about a gallon of 170 degree water ("quickie" meaning slowly pouring gallon of 170 deg. water over the grain bag in a strainer - Sshhh, I think I heard an all-Grainer gap..: ^). Bring to boil, add the extract and molasses (and honey if desired) and.... you know the rest.

For a partial mash, this beer is simple and yielding. All variations have worked wonderfully (ie, with honey and without; with 8# Alexander's pale ale DMS; with 6# Williams Brewing pale DMS + 3# pale DME.. etc..)

English Pale Ale

Category Pale Ale
Recipe Type Extract

Fermentables

4--1/2 lbs. unhopped light dry malt extract
.5 lbs. Dark crystal malt
.5 lbs. Dark brown sugar

Hops

1 oz. Kent Goldings hops (60 minute boil)
.5 oz. Fuggles hops (boil 60 minutes)
.5 oz. Fuggles (boil 30 minutes)
.5 oz. Kent Goldings (10 minute boil)
.5 oz. Kent Goldings (2 minute boil)

Other

1 tsp gypsum or Burton salts

Yeast Whitbread ale yeast (or Munton & Fison or Brewers Choice)

Procedure Notice that the recipe calls for unhopped, light, dry malt extract. Use unhopped extract because you're going to add your own hops. Use light- colored extract because you're going to get some color from the crystal malt. Use dry malt because you can measure it out, unlike syrups. The crystal malt should be cracked. Your homebrew supply store can do that for you. Steep the crystal malt for 30 minutes in your water at 150 degrees F. Then strain the husks out, bring the water to boil, add the gypsum or salt, and add the dry malt. After the wort has been boiling for 10 minutes, add the first hops and follow the hop schedule indicated above. Hops are English hops. Brown sugar can be added as soon as the boil starts. If you use dry packaged yeast, use the above brands. Others are lousy! If you like the recipe, vary only the yeast, and you get a somewhat different beer next time! Whitbred dry yeast and Wyeast "British" ale are the same yeast.

Erik's American IPA #1

Category India Pale Ale
Recipe Type Partial Mash

Fermentables

4.25 lbs. M&F Bulk Pale LME (added at 25 minutes)
 6 lbs. American Pale 2-row
 0.75 lbs. 60L American Crystal
0.25 lbs. Carapils

Hops

0.5 oz. Nugget @40
0.33 oz. Cascade @0
0.5 oz. Nugget Hops (11.8%AA) @100 minutes to end
0.5 oz. Cascade (6.5% AA) @30
0.5 oz. Cascade @15
0.5 oz. Cascade @8   1-1/2 oz. Cascade (dry hop)
.5 oz. Nugget (dry hop)

Yeast Wyeast 1028 London Ale

Procedure I used 1 quart of water per lb of grain (7 quarts total, soft, pre boiled settle water with 2 tsp of Gypsum) I used a short 20 minute protein rest and a long 2 hour mash @156F for some residual body and sweetness in the finished beer.

I only collected about 4.5 gallons of wort because I don't have a big enough brew pot. I was within a point or two of my target OG based on my assumed efficiency of 85% of Dave

Miller's optimal numbers. I boiled about 3.5 gal wort with the hops in a 4 gal pot. In another pot I boiled the remaining sweet wort and added it to the main pot as space became available.

All hops were whole hops from the Hop Source (good hops, good prices, no financial or personal interest). I adjusted my IBU calculations for the estimated SG in the main pot. I assumed a more-or-less linear increase in SG between the SG at the start of the boil and the estimated SG at the time I added all running to the main pot. When calculating the IBUs for the early additions I did not try to take into account the dramatic boost in OG over the last 25 minutes of the boil caused by the addition of the LME.

I cooled the wort over 40 minute's time in a covered kettle in a tub- full of cold water. Yeast was pitched at about 75F. Fermentations proceeded at 60F. Racked to carboy after 5 days, dry hopped for 8 before bottling.

Extract Kolsch

Category German Ale
Recipe Type Extract

Fermentables
6.00 lb. Light Dry Malt Extract
0.25 lb. Wheat

Hops
1.25 oz. Hallertau 3.1% 15 min
0.50 oz. Czech Saaz 3.5% dry hopped
0.50 oz. Hallertau 3.1% dry hopped

Other
0.50 oz. Northern-Br. 6.9% 75 min
0.75 oz. American Spalt 4.0% 15 min
1 tsp of Irish Moss

Yeast Kolsch Wyeast

Procedure The .25lb. crushed wheat grain was placed in a grain bag, put in the cold water (2.5 gallons), and raised to 165 degrees where it steeped for 10 minutes. I then raised the it to a boil, added the boiling hops (the Northern) and the DME. After 60 minutes I added the flavor hops (.75 oz. of the spalt and 1.25 oz. of the Hallertau) and 1 teaspoon of Irish Moss. I then let this boil for 15 minutes (75 minutes total).

I then put in my primary and added the Kolsch Wyeast (liquid, natch). This is an interesting yeast. I let it ferment at around 62-64 for about 1 1/2 weeks, until it seemed just about done. I then threw it into the fridge at 42 degrees for about 2 weeks. When I took it out, the yeast appeared upset by the sudden temperature change and it fermented rather energetically for about 1/2 day or so, and then it slowed down. I took a specific gravity and it was 1.08. Done. (I screwed up the starting gravity. Ooops). I primed and bottled. Let it sit for two weeks, then placed it in the fridge. Let it sit in the fridge about 1 week before drinking, and MMMMMMMMMMMM..... good   stuff

First All Grain

Category Pale Ale
Recipe Type All Grain

Fermentables
6 lbs. Klages [I would boost this to 8+. --Ed.]
1 lb Crystal malt
1 lb light DME (due to low extraction rate) [... and drop this.]
1 oz. Chocolate malt

Hops
1 oz. Hallertauer 8.5% for boiling
1 oz. Cascade 3% last 10 min of boil

Other

1 tsp Irish Moss (last 15 min.. Didn't re-hydrate)

Yeast 20 oz. of starter. Wyeast #1028 (the pack was over a year old and took 6 days

Procedure I used about 3 gallons of mash water, making for a soupy mash. Boosted the temperature of the mash to 155 without any protein rest. I had used about 3 teaspoons of gypsum to get the mash down to a PH of about 5.0.

Put in an insulated box for 2 1/2 hours. Ending temp was 145. The requirement was for two hours, but getting the sparge water ready took longer than I wanted. Then I boosted to 168 degrees for mash-out. (The iodine test showed complete conversion).

For the sparge water, I used an 8% Phosphoric acid solution to acidify 6 gallons of hot tap water. After 2 tsps, my PH strips looked like they were still above 6.0. Then, on the 3rd teaspoon, the PH abruptly changed, and the test strips remained yellow, indicating that it was now very acidic. I had to add about 3 more gallons of water before it got back up to about 5.0.

I was expecting just a slow trickle for the sparge, but once I opened the spigot on my later turn, the wort hissed out. (Used the cylindrical cooler with a sparge bag on the SS vegetable strainer) It never did slow to a trickle as I was expecting. I slowed the flow of the output and input so that the sparge would take about an hour. (The water was 168 degrees, Re-circulated 1st run until clear) NOTE: I don't think the water was leaking thru the sides of the sparge bag, and it looked like it *was* filtering through the grain bed OK, which was always held in suspension.

Collected about 8 gallons of wort (pH of the running never dropped below 5.8 even though the gravity dropped to about 1.010) and boiled for 90 minutes. A gravity reading before the boil showed only about 1.020 (granted, it was 8 gallons) prompting me to add 1 lbs DME. I thought I had boiled down to 5 gallons, but was actually 6. (Haven't put any sort of volume markings in my Snaky keg boiler yet). Used a CF chiller, shook the 6 1/2 gal car-boy for about 5 minutes to oxygenate and pitched yeast. FG was only 1.032 at 60 deg F

Flaherty's Red

Category Pale Ale
Recipe Type All Grain

Fermentables
1 ea potatoes, peeled and grated

Hops
1 oz. Cascade hops boiling
1 oz. Fuggle hops (finish)

Yeast WYeast European Ale

Flat Tyre

Category Belgian Ale
Recipe Type Extract

Fermentables
6 lbs. Light extract
2 lbs. Amber extract
.5 lb 20L crystal
.5 lb dextrine malt (carapils)
Scant 3/4 cup of corn sugar for priming

Hops
1 oz. Chinook hops
1 oz. Cascade hops

Yeast Wyeast 1056 American (aka Chico)

Procedure Add 1.5 gallons cold water and the grains (in a bag) to your boiling pot. Spend about 30 mins bringing the water to a boil. I use medium high on my generic electric range, high boils too quickly and doesn't give the grains enough soaking time.

Remove the grain bag just before the water boils.

Groovy Time Pale Ale

Category Pale Ale
Recipe Type Extract

Fermentables
.5 lb 120L Crystal Malt
6.6 lb Home Brewery Light Malt Extract (3.3 hopped, 3.3 unhopped)
.75 cup corn sugar (priming)

Hops
1.5 oz. Saaz Hops
.333 oz. Fuggles Hops
.5 oz. Cascades Hops

Yeast Doric dry ale yeast

Procedure In 2 Gallons of Water I Added the cracked Crystal Malt, heated and removed at 170 deg. f (Approx 30 min) Added the hopped and unhopped extract along with 1 oz. of the Saaz and .333 Fuggles at beginning of boil (boiled for 75 min total) Added .5 oz. Saaz last 10 minutes Added .5 oz. Cascades then cut off the heat.
Had made a yeast starter of 4 tubes of brewing sugar in 2 cups of water (boiled) then poured into the sanitized fresh bottle with an airlock on top, when it reached 90 deg. f I pitched (2) 5 gram packs of Doric dry ale yeast, it was bubbling like crazy when I pitched it about 45 minutes after pitching the yeast into the bottle.

I used Crystal Springs bottled spring water, nasty water in Smyrna Tennessee.

Hazelnut Brown

Category Brown Ale
Recipe Type Extract

Fermentables

6.6 lbs. N.W. Gold liq. extract
.5 lb. M&F pale ale malt
.5 lb. M&F crystal malt (60 L?)
1 lb. Cara-pils

Hops

1.5 oz. Willamette (or Fuggle) 60 min. boil
1 oz. Willamette or Fuggle (aroma) 5 minute steep

Other

1 tsp Irish moss (15 min room end)
1.5 bottles All Natural Hazelnut Flavoring at bottling
2 tsp. Gypsum

Yeast Wyeast British Ale

Procedure Mash grain at 160 F.

Heavy Weather

Category Pale Ale
Recipe Type Extract

Fermentables

1 can Munton's York shire bitter
2 lbs. Light malt extract
1 lb dark malt extract

Hops

1 oz. Goldings hops

Other
.25 tsp Irish moss
1 whole vanilla bean (use 1/2 if you hate a sweetish beer)

Yeast Munton's ale yeast

Procedure Boil with 1 1/2 gals H2O for 60 mins. Add 1/2 the hops, Irish moss, and vanilla bean at 15 mins before end of boil. Toss the rest of the hops at 3 mins before done boiling. Have 3 1/2 gals chilled H20 in the fermenter and filter in the world through a strainer. Get the batch to 75f or so and pitch the yeast (rehydrated). Agitate the wort, stick on the airlock, and lock it away in the fridge (35f) for 9 days. Prime w/ 3/4 cup corn sugar and bottle away. It was quite drinkable after 2 weeks in bottles, but the longer it stays there, the better it gets.

Heavyside Ale

Category Scottish Ale
Recipe Type Extract

Fermentables
3.5 lbs. Glenbrew heavy 80 ale kit
2--1/4 lbs. Laaglander dark, dry extract
.5 lbs. Crushed crystal malt (20L)

Hops
1 oz. Northern Brewer hops (steep last 10 minutes)

Yeast 2 packages dry ale yeast (from kit)

Procedure Prepare yeast by reconstituting in 16 ounces, warm tap water in a jar before brewing begins. Slowly bring 1 quart cold tap water with 1/2 pound crystal malt to a boil, about 30 minutes. Remove spent grains by pouring the liquid through a strainer into the main brew pot and sparging with

1 quart boiling water. Add 3 US pints of water to brew pot and bring to a boil. Add can and dry extract and boil for 15 minutes. Steep hop pellets in hop bag for 10 minutes with heat off, then remove hops and pour concentrated wort into the fermenter. Since I've marked the outside of the fermenter in gallon increments, I then added cold water to raise the level to the 5 gallon line. After cooling I pitched the yeast, sealed it up, and attached the fermentation lock. After less than 7 hours, the wort was bubbling like mad. Prime with 1 cup dark extract when finished.

Jim's 90 Schilling Scotch Ale

Category Scottish Ale
Recipe Type All Grain

Fermentables

8 Lbs. British Pale Ale Malt 2-row 1 Lb Carapils Malt
1 Lb Peated Malt 1 Lb Biscuit Malt
1 Lb 90L Crystal Malt
 3 oz. Roasted Barley
1 2/3 cup gold dry malt for bottling

Hops
3 oz. Kent Goldings 5% alpha acid leaf hops 2 oz. Fuggles 4% alpha acid plug hops

Other
3 tsp Irish moss
10 Gallons artesian drinking water

Yeast #1728 WYeast Scottish ale liquid yeast

Procedure PREPARATION: Prepare a 2-3 quart yeast starter ahead of time. Scotch ale needs a high pitching rate.

MASH: Use a single step infusion mash for all 12 lbs. of grain. Mill grains and add to 3 gallons Artesian water at 180 degrees F in the mash turn. Mash should stabilize at ~158 degrees F. The mash should be on the thick side. Hold temp at about 158 degrees F for

90 minutes for conversion. Stir in the roasted barley about 5 minutes before sparging. Sparge with 5 gallons water initially at 180 degrees F. This will stop conversion for the mash out. Sparge slowly for about 45 minutes. You should get about 5.5-6.0 gallons of wort.

BOIL: Total boil time 90 minutes. Bring to a boil rapidly and stir after 2-3 minutes. This will lightly caramelize the wort to enhance the flavor. Add all 5 ozs. of hops. Scotch ale does not have a flavor or aroma hop profile. Keep a rolling boil and stir well for better hop utilization. You will lose about 1 gallon of water to evaporation. Add Irish moss about 15 minutes before the end of the boil. Cool in cold water sink, bath or wort chiller. Filter into primary fermenter and cool to 75 deg. F.

FERMENT: Pitch yeast starter. Rack to secondary after 5-8 days. Leave in secondary until fermentation is complete. Bottle and condition at ~60 degrees F for six to eight weeks.

John's Raspberry Ale

Category Fruit Beers
Recipe Type Extract

Fermentables
6 lbs. Williams' English Light malt extract
.5 lbs. Crystal malt (unknown Lovibond)
4 lbs. Raspberries

Hops
2 oz. Hallertauer hops (4.0 AA%) (45 minutes)
.5 oz. Hallertauer hops (4.0 AA%) (5 minutes)

Yeast Wyeast liquid yeast (London ale)

Procedure Prepare 1 quart starter two nights before. Purchase some fresh raspberries (if possible. Try local farmer's market). The freeze raspberries night before brewing to break down cell walls. Pre-boil some water. Cooled some and freeze some. Prepare wort as usual by steeping crystal malt in 150-160F water while the brew pot water is heating up and sparg into the brew pot. Boil about an hour. Add 2 ounces Hallertau at 15 minutes and another 1/2 ounces at end of boil. At the end of the boil, toss all the raspberries into the brew pot and let sit for fifteen minutes. The wort was pretty cool by then. Toss *everything* into the fermenter. (With the raspberries in there, I figured I couldn't get any S.G. readings, so I didn't try.)

Kolsch 1

Category German Ale
Recipe Type Extract

Fermentables
4 lb can Alexander's Pale Malt Extract
1.4 lb can Alexander's Pale Malt Extract "Kicker"
1 lb rice syrup solids

Hops
1 oz. Liberty hop pellets (5.2%), boiling, 45-60 minutes
1/3 oz. Saaz hop pellets (54.%), flavor, 15 minutes
2/3 oz. Saaz hop pellets (5.4%), finishing, 5 minutes

Other
1 tsp Irish moss, 20 minutes (optional)

Yeast Wyeast 1007 "German Ale" yeast - started 24 hours ahead

Procedure Bring 5 gallons of water to a boil, remove heat, dissolve malt and rice syrup solids, and bring back to a boil. Add boiling hops and boil for 30-45 minutes. Add Irish moss. Add flavor hops and boil for 10 more minutes, add finish hops and boil for 5 more minutes. Remove heat and cool wort as rapidly as possible. Transfer to carboy, pitch yeast and mix/aerate vigorously. Ferment it (primary only) for 10 days at 70-75F.

Prime with 3/4 cup (5 oz) corn sugar dissolved in 2 cups (16 oz) of boiling water, at bottling time. The bottle should be conditioned in 7 to 10 days.

Notes: By boiling in a short time will help keep the color light, but will decrease hops character and protein precipitation. BE WARNED! Wyeast 1007 ferments vigorously, even volcanically. Make sure that you have enough head space in your carboy, or use a large diameter blow off tube.

Kolsch 2

Category German Ale
Recipe Type All Grain

Fermentables
6 lbs. U.S. 2--row malt
1 lb. Vienna malt
1 lb. Wheat malt
.25 lbs. Light crystal malt (10 L.)

Hops
1 oz. Hallertauer (2.9% alpha) (60 minute boil)
1 oz. Hallertauer (30 minute boil)
.25 oz. Tettnanger (3.8% alpha) (15 minute boil)
.25 oz. Tettnanger (2 minute boil)

Yeast Wyeast European ale yeast

Procedure I'm assuming 80% extraction efficiency. The hop schedule broadly follows the German method, and you can substitute Perle or Spalt, and mix and match however you want.

Following Fred Eckhardt's description of Widmer's mash sequence, mash in at 122 degrees F and hold for 30 to 45 minutes, and then raise to 158 degrees F for starch conversion. Following conversion, raise to 170 degrees F for mash out and hold for 10 minutes.

Primary fermentation should be done in the mid-60s. This beer benefits from cold-conditioning, so rack to secondary and "lager" at 40 degrees for a couple weeks.

Remove the pot from the heat (to prevent scorching) and add the extract.

Replace on the heat and add 3/4 oz. Chinook hops - boil for 60 min.

Add 1 oz. Cascades for the last 15 minutes of the boil.

Cool to about 100F (chiller, ice bath, snow drift or divine intervention) Add cooled wort to 3 gallons cold water in your primary fermenter.

When the temp is less than 80F (should be by now) add the yeast and shake the snot out of it, um, I mean, aerate the wort.

When fermentation is complete, make a 'hop tea' by boiling the remaining 1/4 oz. Chinook hops (I know, not a classic aroma hop) with your priming sugar. Bottle, wait at least three weeks and enjoy.

Liberty Ale Success

Category India Pale Ale R
Recipe Type Extract

Fermentables
8 lbs. Munton and Fisons light malt extract
. 5 lb 40L Crystal Malt
.5 lb Munich Malt

.5 lb Cara Pils Malt

Hops
1.5 oz. Fuggles Hops (bittering)
3.5 oz. Cascade Hops (flavor, aroma, dry-hop etc)

Yeast Wyeast 1056 American Ale yeast culture

Procedure Mash the Crystal, Munich and Cara Pils malts in a couple of quarts of 150 degrees (all degrees in Fahrenheit, sorry non-US) water for about 30 minutes. Raise the temperature to 158 degrees, and hold it for 15 minutes. Raise the temperature to 168 degrees briefly, then sparge with another quart or two of 170 degree water. Add a gallon of water to mash, then boil it with the malt extract for 60 minutes. At the beginning of the boil, add 1.5 oz. Fuggles Hops. At 30 minutes, add 1 oz. Cascades. At 10 minutes, add 1/2 oz. Cascades. At the end of the boil, turn off the burner and add 1/2 oz. of Cascades. Let this steep for 5-10 minutes. Cool and strain (if you aren't using hop bags) into the fermenter. Pitch yeast and top off with cold water. Rack it in 1 week, and add 1.5 oz. Cascades to the secondary fermenter. Wait one more week and bottle with 3/4 cups corn sugar. Wait one more week and serve very cold.

Minnesota Wild Rice Amber
Category Amber Ale
Recipe Type Extract

Fermentables
3.1 lbs. Superbrau light unhopped malt extract syrup 2 lbs. Gold dry malt extract (spray malt)
.5 lbs. 2-row malted barley
.5 lbs. Special roast barley
.5 lbs. Wild rice

Hops
.5 oz. Chinook hop pellets
.5 oz. Willamette hop pellets

Yeast 1 pack Windsor ale yeast (Canadian)

Procedure I put all the grains into a saucepan with enough hot water to cover, and kept it hot (not boiling) while stirring periodically for about an hour. The malted barley was supposed to supply enough enzymes to convert the wild rice starches into sugars. I don't know how well it worked, but the resulting wort was amber and sweet.

I sparged it into a **brew pot** by dumping the grains into a colander and running a bit of hot water through. I did recalculate once, but it was a clumsy process and I wouldn't swear that I did a thorough job of either extracting or filtering.

I added the extracts and the boiling hops (the latter in a bag), and boiled it for a little over half an hour, then added the aromatic hops while I prepared the fermenter. This was the first time I used a hop bag. I don't know if it cuts down on the extraction from the pellets or not. I do know that it cut down on the mess in the fermenter.

I poured the hot wort into the fermenter, added three or four gallons of very cold water and pitched the yeast.

Mom's Special Ale

Category Pale Ale
Recipe Type Extract

Fermentables

6 lbs. English Light syrup malt extract
2 lbs. English Light dry mail extract

2.2 lbs. Morgan's Master Blend Caramalt syrup malt extract
1 lbs. 80 L. Crystal malt

Hops
2.5 oz. Fuggle hops (boil)
1 oz. Challenger hops (finishing)
1 oz. Perle (7.3% alpha) hops (aroma)

Other
1 tsp. Irish Moss
10 cinnamon sticks (4"-5")
.75 cup corn sugar (priming)

Yeast Wyeast #1968 London ESB yeast

Procedure Place 80 L. crystal malt in straining bag and suspend in 3 gallons cold water, bring to boil. Once water comes to boil, remove spent crystal malt grains and feed to awaiting birds outside. Add all syrup and dry malt extracts, along with Fuggle hops in the boil. Boil for 30 minutes, then stir in Irish moss. Boil for an additional 25 minutes, then stir in Challenger hops. Boil for 5 more minutes, then remove pot from the flame. Cool to 100 degrees F., then mix into fermenter holding 2 gallons cold water, top until 5 gallons total capacity. Pitch with Wyeast #1968 yeast. Add cinnamon sticks to primary fermenter and let sit for 2 weeks. Rack to secondary fermenter and dry hop with Perle hops (pellets), let sit for 1 week. Prime with corn sugar and bottle.

Mongrel Ale (Smoked)
Category Smoked Beer
Recipe Type Extract

Fermentables

1 lb smoked crystal (60 L)
.5 lb smoked pale English 2-row

1 lb Munich malt
3 lbs. Amber M&F dried malt extract
2 lbs. Light M&F dried malt extract
.75 cup corn sugar (priming)

Hops
.5 oz. Galena pellets (alpha = 12.0; 60 min.)
.5 oz. Hallertauer pellets (alpha = 4.5; 15 min.)
.5 oz. Hallertauer pellets (alpha = 4.5; 1 min.)

Other
.5 tsp Irish Moss (15 min.)

Yeast Wyeast 1007: German Ale

Procedure Using a water smoker, I smoked the crystal and pale malt at about 170F over hickory wood for 3-4 hours using heavy smoke. When finished, the malt smelled smoke, but didn't taste smoky, so I took half the crystal and gave it another 3-4 hours. This smelled REALLY smoky, but still didn't taste smoky.

On brew day, I cracked all grains and steeped them in 3 qts. of water for 45 minutes at 150-155F. I sparged with 1 (US) gallon of 170F water, recalculating twice (I wanted that smoke, and was willing to get a few more tannins). I added the runoff and extracts to the kettle, and topped up to 5 and 1/2 to 6 gallons of water. I boiled 65 minutes, adding the hops and Irish Moss as shown. I calculated the IBUs to be about 30, but the finished product doesn't taste 30 IBUs worth of bitter (maybe my calculations were off; also my crude measuring instruments mean that those quantities on the hops are, er, approximate). Cooled with an immersion chiller and pitched the yeast from a starter

Northern Lights

Category Pale Ale

Recipe Type All Grain
Fermentables
13 lbs. 2--row pale malted barley
2 lbs. 20L crystal malt
1 lb. Wheat malt

Hops
2 oz. Cascade leaf hops (boil)
.5 oz. Perle leaf hops (boil)
.5 oz. Fuggles leaf hops (boil)
1 oz. Chinook leaf hops (boil)
.5 oz. Chinook leaf hops (finish)
.5 oz. Fuggles leaf hops (finish)
1 oz. Northern Brewer hops pellets (dry hop in

Other
1 lb. Corn flakes

Yeast Wyeast German ale yeast #1007
Procedure I did a step mash, following normal procedure.

Old Beulah Wee Export

Category Scottish Ale
Recipe Type All Grain

Fermentables

2 lbs. 2--row Klages malt
.5 lbs. Crystal malt (60L)
.25 lbs. Black patent malt
.25 lbs. Flaked barley
5 lbs. Amber malt extract syrup (American Classic)
1 lb. Dark brown sugar
.75 cup corn sugar (bottling)

Hops

1 oz. Northern Brewer hop pellets (6.5% alpha)
2 oz. Fuggles hop pellets (4.5% alpha)

Other

3 tsp gypsum
.25 tsp Irish moss

Yeast Wyeast #1028 London Ale yeast

Procedure Step mash. Crush grains and add to 3 quarts
water (with gypsum dissolved) at 130F. Maintain mash
temperature at 125 for 30 min (protein rest). Add 3 quarts of
boiling water to mash and maintain temperature at 158 for 1
hour (saccharification rest). Drain wort and sparge grains
with 5 quarts water at 170. Add to the wort in the **brew pot**
the malt extract and brown sugar. Bring to a boil. After 30
minutes of boil, add 1/2 ounce of Northern Brewer hops and
1/2 ounce of Fuggles hops. After 15 more minutes, add an
additional 1/2 ounce of each hop. Boil for a total of 1- -1/2
hours. Ten minutes before the end of the boil, add the Irish
moss. Five minutes before the end of the boil, add 1 ounce of

Fuggles hops (for aroma). Cool the wort with a wort chiller and add to the primary fermenter with sufficient water to make 5 gallons. Pitch yeast when temp of wort is below 75. Ferment at 65 for 5 days. Rack to secondary and ferment for 15 more days at 65. Bulk prime with corn sugar before bottling.

Pale Ale

Category Pale Ale
Recipe Type Extract

Fermentables
3.3 lbs. Light M&F DME
3 lbs. Light unhopped M&F malt extract
1 lb. Crystal malt

Hops
2 oz. Willamette hops

Yeast Wyeast #1007

Procedure Started yeast 48 hours prior to brewing. Used 1 cup DME boiled in 2 cups water for primer.
1 ounce Willamette at start of boil 1, ounce at end. Boiled 1/2 hour, sat 1/2 hour, strained into primary, pitched yeast, fermented at 78 in primary for 1 week, secondary for 2 weeks. Use bottled water because my water has a high concentration of calcium and no chlorine.

Pyle Style Pale Ale

Category Pale Ale
Recipe Type All Grain

Fermentables
5.00 lb American pale malt from Briess
4.00 lb English pale malt from Hugh Baird
0.75 lb Belgian crystal malt

Hops
1.00 oz. Mt. Hood pellets (a=3. 9)
1.00 oz. Cascade pellets (a=5. 1)
0.60 oz. Cascade leaf hops (a=5. 6)

Other
1.00 tsp Irish moss (added in the last 10 minutes of boil)
0.75 cup corn sugar for bottling

Yeast 1056 Wyeast American Ale yeast dated 6/23/93

Procedure Mash water was 9 quarts of 168F water poured into a room temperature 48 quart rectangular cooler mash/later turn. Doughed in pale malts only. Mash-in temperature was 150F after stabilizing. Mashed at 145-155 (added 1 quart of 180F water when the temp dropped to 145F). Conversion complete in one hour. Crystal was added at mash-out. Dumped 20 quarts of 180F water into turn and stirred (mash out and batch sparge in one step). Sparge was very slow, nearly stuck twice, so I back flushed the copper manifold to loosen it up (need to adjust my grain mill!). Start of boil, the volume was around 32 quarts. Boiled down to 22 qts. at 1.045. Points of extract = (45pts. * 5.5 gal.) / 9.75 lbs. = 25 pts/lb/gal.

Hopping schedule:
60 min: 0.50 oz. MH IBU = 8.3
30 0.50 MH 4.5
0.50 caps 5.8

Richard's Red

Category Pale Ale
Recipe Type Extract

Fermentables
1 lb Munich
1 lb dark crystal

.75 lb cara pils
1 lb toasted 2-row
.25 lb roast barley
3.5 lbs. Light dry malt extract
1.5 oz. Oak chips

Hops
1.3 oz. Olympic hops at boil
2/3 oz. Cascade hops when heat cuts

Yeast Irish ale yeast

Procedure Toast the 2-row grain for 10 minutes in an oven preheated at 350 before crushing.

Crush all the grain.

Put the 4 lbs. of grain in a grain bag in 4 gal water. If you must use multiple bags, make sure each bag has its proportion of Munich malt; this is where the enzymes are.

Heat the water to 160 and maintain for an hour and a half. Every 10 minutes or so wring out the grain bag, & stir it around. This may be cut to as short as an one-half hour if you use an iodine test and it confirms conversion.

Wringer out the grain and put it into a colander (sp?), sieve, or strainer over the water. Slowly pour another gallon (or whatever it takes to get to 5 gallons, depending upon how much you boil off, have already boiled, etc.) of 170 degree water through it to wash off remaining sugars.

Raise to boil, add hops and extract as usual.

Steam the oak chips sterilize them--I put a bit of water into a pan, and hold them above in a strainer with a lid over it for about 10 minutes.

Toss the hops in the fermenter along with the wort, & add the oak as well (I suggest leaving them all in cheesecloth bags). Transfer the oak chips to your secondary as well. If you use a keg, toss them in.

10 0.50 Cp 2.5
Dry 0.60 Cl 1.0 (leave on for 10 days)

Approximate Total IBU = 22.1 (Balanced beer at 1.045 = 20 IBU)

A note about hopping: I was attempting to get most of my IBUs later in the boil to reduce some back of the tongue bitterness. I wanted this to be a hop flavored beer, rather than just have bitterness to balance the malt. On most beers I try for 50-60% of the bitterness at the 60 minute addition, but as you can see, I did not do that here. I achieved my goal I think (see tasting notes).

Full fermentation in 12 hours, high krauesen in 36 hours. Dry hops were just thrown on top of beer in secondary.

Rick's Wicked Summer Ale

Category Pale Ale
Recipe Type All Grain

Fermentables
4 lbs. American 2-row pale malt
3 lbs. American 6-row pale malt (had some sitting around)
3 lbs. Wheat malt
.5 cup crystal malt (40L)

Hops
1 oz. Cascade pellets (6.3%AAU)
.5 oz. Tettneng pellets -flavor-(4.5%AAU)

Other

Grated lemon peel from 2 lemons (do *not* use the bitter white pith)
Juice from 2 lemons
Yeast Wyeast 1056 500ml starter

Procedure Step-mash: Add 2.25 gal of 54degC water to crushed grains and stabilize to 50-51degC for 30 min. Add 1.25 gallons of 93degC water to bring temp to 65degC; hold there for 90 min. Mash out, sparge, etc.

Bring wort to a boil and add Cascade hops. After 30 min, add 1/2 ounce tettnteg hops, lemon peel, and lemon juice. Boil for another 30 min or so until volume is about 6 gallons. Chill wort, put into the fermenter, and let the trub settle out for a few hours, transfer clear wort to a sanitized glass carboy, and pitch yeast.

OG= 1.052 (for a lighter beer, bring volume to six gallons)

When bottling, add 3/4 cup corn sugar and juice and zest from 2 lemons.

Special Bitter #9

Category Pale Ale
Recipe Type All Grain

Fermentables
7 lbs. 2-row pale malt 1 lb. Crystal malt (60 L.)
.5 lbs. Wheat malt
1 oz. Black patent malt

Hops

1 oz. Centennial hops (10.9% alpha)

Yeast Wyeast 1028

Procedure Mash in: 12 qt. @ 140F Mash: 60 min. @ 150-156 F pH 5.2 Mash out: 15 min. @ 170F

Sparge: 5 gal. Acidified to pH 5.8 w/lactic acid. Boil: 90 minutes Hops: 1 addition, 45 min. from end.

I used the theoretical values in Miller's Complete Handbook of Home Brewing, and the SG points avail- abilities of the grain bill were 290. Multiply 58 by 5 and be amazed as I was! Yes, I got 100% of theoretical extraction, and only sparged 5 gal.! How? I'll describe my sparge procedure this time, because I believe herein lies the key.

For lautering, I use the bucket in bucket turn. I'd suspect that it's the same as many other brewers use. It isn't insulated, or anything fancy. Sparge water was acidified with lactic acid ala Miller. Here's the difference. I recalculated the initial runoff for the equivalent of 6 gal. Then I began the sparge with 1/2 of the water heated to 170F and recalculated it once. I finished up with the last 2.5 gal., which was also recalculated once. Total sparge time was about 2.5 hours. The sparge was a good bit longer than usual, but those results!!! The runoff was reheated between recirculations, BTW. The last running had no perceivable tannic taste.

Scotch Ale

Category Scottish Ale
Recipe Type Extract

Fermentables
lb Ireks Munich light LME
2.0 lb Ireks Munich malt (10L?)
0.5 lb M&F crystal malt (60L)
0.5 lb Ireks crystal malt (20L)
 3.0 oz. M&F chocolate malt (350L)
4.0 oz. White wheat malt (2L)

2.0 oz. Hugh Baird peat smoked malt (2L)
4.5 oz. Corn sugar (priming)

Hops
1.0 oz. East Kent Goldings (whole, 60 min boil)
1.0 oz. Fuggles (whole, 15 min boil)

Other
1 tsp Irish moss (rehydrated, 15 min boil)

Yeast Wyeast 1338 (European ale 1 qt starter)

Procedure - mashed all the grains in 4 quarts of 156F water for 1 hour
- sparged with 4 qts of 170F water
- SG of running: 1.036 in ~7 qts
- added LME, made volume up to 3 gal, boiled for 1 hour
- chilled with immersion chiller, aerated, made volume up to 5 gal, aerated some more, pitched 1 quart starter
- fermented at 65 - 68F

I use a grain bag from Williams Brewing (800-759-6025) that is made to fit inside a bucket type lauter turn. It also fits perfectly inside my 3 gallon SS kettle.

To do the mash on my stove, I just heat up the mash water to ~165F (in my kettle) then drop in the grain bag containing the crushed grains. Stir real well, let it sit for a minute, then check the temp. If it's to low (which it will be) either add small amounts of boiling water (1 cup at a time, stir, let it sit for a minute, then check the temp) or add heat with the stove burner on medium heat while gently stirring constantly. After you hit the mash temp, cover it up and let it sit for 1 hour. At the end of the 1 hour, I lift the grain bag just above the surface of the wort and sparge by pouring the sparge water over the grains gently with a measuring cup.

As you can see, my mash setup/technique is pretty simple and doesn't require a lot of extra equipment. I'm not trying to get the max possible extraction from the grains, only the flavor/body that was missing before I started doing these partial mashes.

Since this setup/technique has produced wort that is rather cloudy with grain particles, I've often wondered if it will lead to some astringency in the finished beer. Some of the judges' comments (see below) lead me to believe that this does happen. Kirk Fleming asked about this in HBD #1968. Does this stovetop mashing sound similar to what you do?

Scottish Export

Category Scottish Ale
Recipe Type Extract

Fermentables

6 lbs. Light DME
1 lb. Crystal malt 60L
1/2 lbs. Chocolate malt ~340L
1 lb. Dark brown sugar

Hops

2 oz. Fuggles pelletized hops (~3.5% AAU)

Other

1 tsp Irish Moss
1/2 tsp Burton salts (if needed)

Yeast and a good ale yeast (Wyeast Scotch Ale yeast is preferred)

Procedure Pre-boil and cool 2 gals of water and store in closed carboy. Add 4 gal water to the kettle and heat to 150 deg F. Remove from heat and steep crystal and chocolate malts for 15 minutes. Return to heat and at around 170 deg, remove malts. Add DME, brown sugar, hops, and salts (if necessary). Boil down to ~3.5 gal for 1 hour. During last 15 minutes of boil, add Irish Moss. Cool and add to carboy. Pitch yeast at 70 deg F. Shake well, keep in a dark area at 70 deg F.

Scottish Steamy Ale

Category Scottish Ale
Recipe Type Extract

Fermentables
6 lbs. M&F light, dry extract
1 lb. Scottish crystal malt (40L)

Hops
1 oz. Northern Brewer leaf hops (boil)
.5 oz. Northern Brewer (finish)

Yeast, Brewers Choice American ale yeast

Procedure Boiling hops are put in the kettle for a 55 minute boil. The finishing hops are put in for an additional 5 minutes.

Taken Liberties Ale

Category Pale Ale
Recipe Type Extract

Fermentables
.5 lbs. Crystal malt (60L)
1 cup English 2--row pale malt
7 lbs. Light Munton & Fison dry malt extract
.5 cup corn sugar (priming)

Hops

.5 oz. Galena pellets (12% alpha) 1 oz. Cascade pellets (5.5% alpha) 1 oz. Cascade pellets

Other

.5 oz. Irish moss

Yeast Wyeast American ale #1056

Procedure Cracked grains and steeped in 2 (U.S.) quarts 150-155F water for 45 minutes. Collected runoff and sparged with an additional 1--1/2 gallons 170F water. Added to brew kettle with enough additional water to make 5- -1/2 gallons. Dissolved extract and boiled 65 minutes, adding hops and Irish Moss as shown. Chilled with an immersion chiller down to 70F. Racked off break and pitched onto dregs of the secondary of a previous batch, a la Father Barleywine. Active fermentation in less than 12 hours. O.G. = 1.056; IBU = approximately 33 (not counting the dry hopping, which would have added a point or two). Single-stage blow off fermentation in the low 70's. The primary was 4 days, after which I attached a fermentation lock and dumped in the dry-hopping hops. After another 19 days of secondary, I racked to a Cornelius keg primed with 1/2 cup of corn sugar. After waiting a week or so, I tapped, keeping 20 psi on the keg at all other times.

Tooncinator Motley Cru

Category Belgian Ale
Recipe Type Extract

Fermentables

8 lbs. Briess Wheat/Malt powder (2 big zip locks)
2 lbs. Vienna carapils malt (2 small zip locks)
1 3/4 cups corn sugar

Hops

1 oz. Lublin(?) hops, A=3.1 boil (pellets) 1 oz. Hallertau hops, A=4. 8 boil (pellets)

1 oz. Hallertau hops, A=4.8 finishing (pellets)

Other

.5 oz. Coriander seed (freshly crushed) about 1/2 oz. Dried orange peel (Lawries?)
5 whole cloves (to make me feel good, imperceptible) Crystal bottled water

Yeast 2 packages Red Star Ale yeast

Procedure Crushed and steeped carapils. >30 min @130F, 150F, 170F. Sparged, increased volume to almost 4 gallons, heated and stirred in malt powder. Added hops in 4 portions after boil began, about every 15 minutes until they were all in - boiled another 45 minutes after last addition. Turned off heat, stirred in coriander seed, orange peel and cloves, started the chiller about 2-3 minutes later. Siphoned into carboy, added water to about 5 gallons, pitched yeast directly and shook to aerate. Wort didn't taste unduly strange, kind of hoppy, and not too spicy.

After secondary fermentation was complete I decided it should be hoppier and added the 2nd oz. of Hallertau pellets. 3 days later I reconsidered and racked off the hops. I further decided to test out the scrubbing bubble theory of hops reduction - I boiled 1 cup of corn sugar and steeped another tsp orange peel and added it - got a fairly vigorous fermentation for several more days.

Zulu's Xmas Lager

Category Spiced Beers
Recipe Type Extract

Fermentables
 2--3/4 lbs. Light dry malt extract
2.5 lbs. Light clover honey
1 lb. Crystal malt
.75 cup corn sugar for priming
3.3 lbs. Munton & Fison Light Hopped Malt Syrup

Hops
 2 oz. Cascade hops (4.5% alpha)
1 oz. Cascade hops
.5 oz. Cascade hops
.5 oz. Cascade hops

Other
 2 tsp gypsum (soft water treatment)
2 tsp dried ground ginger
2 tsp dried ground nutmeg
3 tsp dried ground cinnamon
1 ea grated orange
.25 tsp Irish Moss

Yeast

 Procedure Steep crystal malt in brew pot. Remove grains before boil. Add extracts and honey and bring to a boil. Add 2 ounces Cascade at beginning of boil. Add ginger, nutmeg, cinnamon, orange peel, and Irish moss in last 10 minutes. Add 1 ounce of Cascade hops two minutes later. Add 1/2 ounce Cascade in the last 5 minutes and the last 1/2 ounce in the last 2.

CHAPTER 5- STOUT

Sweet Darkness

Category Stout
Recipe Type Extract

Fermentables
7 lbs. Australian light syrup
1 lb. Chocolate malt
1.5 lbs. Black patent
12 oz. Crystal malt **Hops**
2 oz. Kent Goldings hops (whole leaf)

Other
12 oz. Lactose 1 tsp salt
1 tsp citric acid

Yeast yeast

Procedure Bring the wort to boil (water and syrup to make 3 gallons), then add crystal. Boil 10 minutes, then add hops. Boil 5 minutes. Turn off heat and add chocolate and black patent malt in a grain bag. Steep about 10 minutes. Sparge grain bag with about 2 gallons of boiling water. Add lactose. Chill and pitch. When fermented, try priming with 3/4 cup of light dry malt extract.

All Grain Porter / All-Grain Stout

Category Stout
Recipe Type All Grain

Fermentables 3 lbs. Klages
3 lbs. Pale malt (dark)
2 lbs. Pale malt (very light)
2 lbs. Vienna malt

2 lbs. Barley flakes
1 lb. Untied malted barley
8 oz. Roasted barley
8 oz. Black patent

Hops
24 grams Billion hops
30 grams Cascade hops
4 grams Hallertauer hops

Other
8 oz. Chocolate

Yeast Wyeast German ale

Procedure The flaked barley has no husk, so I saw no reason not to grind it finely. Mash in at 130 degrees. Let rest 20 minutes or so. Mash at 150 degrees for 115 minutes. Sparge. Let the spargings settle. What seemed to be 3 or 4" of hot break settled out of the initial spargings! Boil for 2 hours. Add hops as follows:
14 grams bullion and 16 grams cascade (very fresh) for 1:45.
10 g bullion and 14 g cascade for 1:05.
4 grams hallertauer finish.
Chill with an immersion chiller, and strain the wort through the hops. Makes about 5.5 gallons of 1.068

Amy's Stout

Category Stout
Recipe Type All Grain

Fermentables
5.5 lb Hugh Baird Pale Ale malt
0.5 lb Carapils malt (Hugh Baird)
0.5 lb Hugh Baird 50L crystal
1.0 lb flaked oats (McCann's Irish Quick Oats)
0.7 lb roasted barley

Hops

30 Gram BC Kent Goldings flowers (5%) (60 min)
15 Gram Kent Goldings (15 min)
15 Gram Kent Goldings (5 min)

Yeast, Yeast Lab Irish Ale yeast

Procedure Step mash all grains together @61C for 30 min (3 gal strike), 65C for 30 min. (infuse 2qts boiling water). Sparged 5.8 gallons at 1.038.

Yield: 4.7 gallons @ 1.046 (I did add some top-up water during the boil).

Fermented 1 week in glass at 19-22C with a pint starter of YeastLab Irish Ale. FG 1.012.

Bottled with 1/3c corn sugar into 2 5l mini-kegs and 18 bottles.

Baer's Stout

Category Stout
Recipe Type Extract

Fermentables
.25 lbs. Flaked barley
.25 lbs. Medium crystal malt
6 lbs. Dark Australian malt extract
.5 lbs. Dark Australian dry malt
.25 lbs. Black patent malt
.5 cup molasses

Hops

2 oz. Cascade hops (boil)
2/3 oz. Northern Brewer hops (finish)

Yeast Wyeast British ale yeast

Procedure Steep flaked barley and crystal malt for 50 minutes at 153 degrees. Strain and boil 90 minutes. Add 1/3 of boiling hops after 30 minutes. Add black patent and molasses at 45 minutes. After 60 minutes, add 1/3 of boiling hops. At end of boil add remaining hops. Steep. Strain, cool, and ferment.

Basic Stout

Category Stout
Recipe Type Extract

Fermentables
6-8 lbs. Dark malt extract
1/2-1 lbs. Roasted barley
1/2-1 lbs. Black patent malt
Hops
.75 oz. Bittering hops (e.g., Bullion) small amount aromatic hops (optional)

Yeast ale yeast

Procedure To these skeleton ingredients I add other adjuncts, or remove things if the wind blows from the south. A nice beer is made by using only dark malt and black patent malt. A good strong bittering hops is key; Bullion is lovely, as is Nugget or Chinook.

There are no appreciable differences between making stouts and other ales, save the larger quantities of grain. Beware of 9-pound batches as these can blow the lids off fermenters.

Bitch's Brew Oatmeal Stout

Category Stout
Recipe Type Extract

Fermentables
6 lbs. Dark dry malt extract
2 lbs. Amber dry malt extract
1 lb. Crystal malt
.75 lbs. Roasted barley
.5 lbs. Black patent malt 2 cups Quaker Oats

Hops
2 oz. Bullions hop (boiling)
.5 oz. Willammette hope (finishing)

Yeast 2 packages Whitbread Ale Yeast

Procedure Steep the Oats, and the cracked grains for 1/2 hour in cold water. Heat mixture and remove grains as a boil is reached. Throw in malts and make your wort. Boil Bullions for 45 minutes, Willammette for 5-7 minutes. Have fun.

Black Betty

Category Stout
Recipe Type All Grain

Fermentables
13.0 Lbs. 2-row barley
2.0 Lbs. White wheat
1.0 Lbs. Crystal 20L
1.0 Lbs. Black patent

Hops
2.0 oz. Magnum ~ 15%

Yeast Nottingham Dry Yeast

Procedure This is a single step infusion. Allocate the correct amount of water into the pot and dissolve the gypsum into it. I then heat the water to approximately 150 F and add the grains, stirring to achieve a mixture. Then I place the pot (make sure it will fit) into a preheated oven set at about 165 F. Mash for about 1 hour. Note that the times are approximate and that you are controlling it, checking and stirring every 20 minutes or so. Sparge using hot water in the correct amount so that husk tannins are not extracted. Boil with all hops for about 45 minutes. Cool slightly, and split between primary fermenters. Top off with good drinking water. Once the wort cools to yeast friendly temperature, pitch the yeast and ferment. Only primary ferment for at least two weeks, to allow the high gravity to render into alcohol. Bottle as usual and try to keep your sweaty paws off until it matures. Enjoy.

Black Cat Stout #1

Category Stout
Recipe Type Extract

Fermentables

6.6 lbs. Munton & Fison dark extract syrup
1 lb. Munton & Fison dark, dry extract
.5 lbs. Black patent malt
.75 lbs. Crystal malt
.5 lbs. Roasted barley
.5 cup dark molasses

Hops
.75 oz. Willamette hops (boil)
.75 oz. Cascade hops (boil)

Other
1 tsp vanilla

.5 cup French roast coffee

Yeast 2 packs Edme ale yeast

Procedure Brew a pot of coffee with 1/2 cup of French roast coffee. Steep specialty grains in water as it boils. Remove grains. Boil malts, hops, and vanilla 60 minutes. Strain wort into fermenter. Pour in pot of coffee. Add ice water to make 5 gallons. Pitch yeast. Rack to secondary after 3 days. Bottle 23 days later.

Black Gold Stout

Category Stout
Recipe Type Extract

Fermentables

6 lb M&F Dark Extract Syrup
1 lb M&F Dark DME
8 oz. Black Patent Malt
12 oz. Chocolate Malt
12 oz. Crystal Malt
.75 C. Corn sugar for priming

Hops
1 oz. Chinook Hop Pellets (60 min)
.5 oz. Northern Brewer Hop Pellets (60 min)
.5 oz. Northern Brewer Hop Pellets (20 min)

Other
1.5 tsp. Single Fold Pure Vanilla Extract
.75 C. Freshly Brewed Espresso

Yeast EDME dry ale yeast

Procedure For this I used distilled water with 1 Tbsp. water crystals added. Steep specialty grains, then remove. Add vanilla, espresso, and extracts. Boil for an hour and cool. Rack to primary and pitch yeast. Within minutes activity was observed. Within 12 hours active fermentation, *WARNING* after this stage you WILL need to use a blow off rig. The activity subsided after 2 1/2 days, then racked to secondary for 12 days to ensure no bottle bombs! Bottled with corn sugar and aged @room temp for 8 days. It is now 3 weeks in the basement and better than ever.

Broglio's Quaker Stout

Category Stout
Recipe Type Extract

Fermentables
6 lbs. Dry amber extract
1 lb. Crystal malt
.5 lbs. Roasted barley
1 lb. Quaker oats

Hops
 1 oz. Eroica hops (boil)
1 oz. Kent Goldings hops (finish)

Yeast 2 packs Edme ale yeast

Procedure In two gallons of cold water, add crystal, barley, and oatmeal. Steep until water comes to boil. Sparge with about 1 gallon of hot water. Add dry extract. Bring to boil. Add Eroica hops. Boil 45 minutes. In last 5 minutes of boil, add Kent Golding's hops. Cool to about 75 degrees. Transfer to primary and pitch yeast. Have a homebrew and wait.

Cherry Fever Stout
Category Stout
Recipe Type Extract
Here is a great fruit beer recipe! This recipe is designed for the intermediate brewer.

Fermentables
3.3 lbs. John Bull plain dark malt extract syrup
2.5 lbs. Premier Malt hopped flavored light malt extract syrup
1.5 lbs. Plain dark dried malt extract
1 lb. Crystal malt
.5 lbs. Roasted barley
.75 c. Corn sugar or 1 1/4 c. Dried malt extract (for bottling)
.5 lbs. Black patent malt 3 lbs. Sour cherries

Hops
1.5 oz. Northern Brewer hops (boiling): 13 HBU
.5 oz. Willamette hops (finishing)

Other
2 lbs. Choke cherries or substitute with 2 lbs. more sour cherries 8 tsp. Gypsum

Yeast 1-2 pkgs. Ale yeast

Procedure Add the crushed roasted barley, crystal and black patent malts to 1 1/2 gallons of cold water and bring to a boil. When boiling commences, remove the spent grains and add the malt extracts, gypsum and boiling hops and continue to boil for 60 minutes. Add the 5 lbs. of crushed cherries (pits and all) to the hot boiling wort. Turn off heat and let the wort steep for 15 minutes (at temperatures between 160-180 degrees F {71-88 C} in order to pasteurize the cherries. Do not boil. Add the finishing hops 2 minutes before you pour the entire contents into a plastic primary fermenter and cold water. Pitch yeast when cool. After 4-5 days of primary fermentation, rack the fermenting beer into a secondary fermenter. Secondary fermentation should last about 10-14 days longer. Bottle when fermentation is complete.

Chocolate Stout

Category Stout
Recipe Type Partial Mash

Fermentables
2   lb Pale Ale malt
1 lb Munich malt
.5 lb 80L Crystal
.25 lb Chocolate malt
.25 lb Black Patent malt
3.3 lb American Classic Amber extract syrup
3 lb Dutch DME (I don't know the brand, but it is high in dextrins)
.5 lb brown sugar
.5   inch brewers licorice

Hops
1 oz. Brewers gold (8.5 %alpha) hops - bittering

Other
2 oz. Fresh grated ginger
3 oz. Unsweetened baker's chocolate 1 tsp Irish moss

Yeast 2 package dry Whitbread yeast

Procedure 5Q mash water, 2 1/2 (?) G Sparge water, mash in at 138F, brought to 155F for 1 hour., mash out at 168F

Added extracts and sugar and brought to boil. Added the ginger, licorice, chocolate, and hops after boil started. I was afraid that the chocolate would burn on the bottom of the boiler, so I set each 1 oz. piece on my stirring spoon and dipped gently in the wort until they melted.

The real interesting thing about the brew was that after pitching, a thick bubbly layer of stuff formed on the surface of the beer in the carboy almost immediately after fermentation started, and never left, even after I expected the Kraeusen to fall. There was the usual amount of activity in the beer, but never more than an inch of Kraeusen.

The good thing was that after racking to my secondary carboy, I left most of the stuff that was sitting on the surface in my primary, and almost all of the rest in my secondary when I racked to my bottling bucket.

I primed with amber DME, and the results even after only two weeks are wonderful, however, there is still a small layer of this sediment even in the bottle at the surface of the beer.

Clydesdale Stout

Category Stout
Recipe Type All Grain

Fermentables
300 g Roasted Barley
300 g Chocolate Malt
600 g Crystal Malt (I've been using a fairly low lovibond crystal) 500 g Rolled Oats
2 kg pale malt
Hops
50 g Northern Brewer (boil 60min) 15 g Northern Brewer (boil 15min) 10 g Northern Brewer (end of boil)

Other
.5 teaspoon Irish moss

Yeast Wyeast Irish ale yeast

Procedure Infusion mash this stuff for about 45min., initial strike temp. is 156 F. Do decoctions as necessary to maintain temp. and then to mash out.

After sparging, etc. add about 2kg dark malt extract powder and 250g demerarra sugar plus the hops (all pellets).

No hops strained out or racking off trub. That's right, everybody into the pool. Top up to about 22 L or so. Pitch with Wyeast Irish Ale yeast starter.

Coffee Stout

Category Stout
Recipe Type Extract

Fermentables
6 lb Stone Mountain Brewery amber malt syrup
3 lb Geordie light DME
1 lb crystal malt 10L 8 oz. chocolate malt
2 oz. Roasted barley

Hops
6 oz. Cascade hops (5.2% AA), bittering
1 oz. Cascade hops, flavoring and aroma

Other
8 oz. Italian espresso beans

Yeast 15 g. Windsor dried ale yeast

Procedure Ground specialty malts and steeped in 1 1/2 gal. Cold water. Brought water up to temp and held at 150 - 160 deg F for 1/2 hour. Added extracts, brought to boil and added bittering hops. Boiled for 1 hour. Added 1/2 oz. Hops and ground coffee 10 minutes before end of boil, added 1/2 oz. hops at end of boil. OG 1.070. Kegged 18 January 1996; FG

1.034 (estimated alcohol, 5.9% abs). Tapped keg 25 February 1996.

Coffee Stout

Category Stout
Recipe Type Extract

Fermentables
1 can Stout extract
6 lbs. Dark Dutch bulk extract
1 lb. Chocolate malt
1 lb. Crystal malt
.75 cup brown sugar (priming)

Hops
1 oz. Fuggles hops (bittering)
1 oz. Fuggles hops (flavoring)

Other
12 cups coffee (see note in Procedure)

Yeast 1 package of Wyeast #1084

Procedure Heat water to 160 degrees and steep grains.
Remove grains and heat to boiling. Add extracts and coffee
and heat to boil. Add bittering hops and boil for 40 minutes.
Add flavoring hops and boil for 20 minutes. Cool and pitch
yeast (I used a starter). Rack to secondary when active
fermentation subsides. Leave in secondary 3-4 weeks. When
ready to bottle boil the brown sugar with a pint of water for
priming. This came out with the coffee a bit strong. Next time
I try this I'll probably cut back to 6 to 8 cups of coffee.

Colorado Crankcase Stout

Category Stout
Recipe Type Extract

Fermentables
3.3 lbs. Edme SFX dark malt extract
3.3 lbs. John Bull dark malt extract
2 lbs. Amber dry malt extract
1 lb. Crystal malt
1 lb. Roasted barley 1 lb. Chocolate malt
.75 lbs. Black patent malt
.5 stick brewer's licorice

Hops
2 oz. Brewers Gold hops
2 oz. Fuggles hops

Other
.5 lbs. French roast coffee beans

Yeast Wyeast #1028: British ale

Procedure Steep grains in water while heating. Remove grains just before boiling. During the boil, add licorice and extract. Add 1 ounce of Brewer's Gold for 60 minutes, 1 ounce for 45 minutes, and 1 ounce of Fuggles for 30 minutes. Cool wort and pitch yeast. Add ungrounded coffee beans and remaining ounce of Fuggles. The next day skim off all crud, including coffee beans and hops. One day later, rack to secondary. Ferment three weeks and bottle.

Cottage Coffee Stout

Category Stout
Recipe Type Extract
Sweet stout with a chocolate aroma and a well balanced, low hopped smooth coffee taste.

Fermentables

3.0 kg Dark Malt Extract (2 cans x 3.3 lbs.)
1.0 Lbs. Crystal Malt
0.5 Lbs. Chocolate Malt
0.5 Lbs. Black Patent Malt
1.25 Cup Light DME (priming)

Hops

1.0 oz. Kent Golding 5.5% AA (bittering)
0.5 oz. Fuggles 4.7% AA (bittering)
0.5 oz. Fuggles (flavoring)

Other

0.5 Lbs. Lactose
0.5 Lbs. Hawaiian Chocolate Coffee Beans crushed not ground (or your favorite Java blend)

Yeast Wyeast #1084 Irish Ale

Procedure Steep grains in 1 1/2 gal water at 155 F for 15-20 min. Remove and sparge grains with 1/2 gal water bringing brew to 2 gal total. Stir in malt extract and bittering hops, boil 1 hour. Dissolve lactose in 1 quart water. Add flavor hops and lactose last 15 min of boil. After full boil, remove from heat and steep coffee beans for 15-20 min. Cool wort and pitch yeast. Ferment in primary 5 days, secondary 15 days. Bottle using DME and condition 4-6 weeks. Enjoy.

Crankcase Stout

Category Stout
Recipe Type Extract

Fermentables
1 lb. Crushed crystal malt
1 lb. Crushed roasted barley
1.5 lbs. Crushed black patent malt
9 lbs. Munton & Fison dark, dry malt extract
1 can John Bull dark hopped malt extract
2 inches brewers licorice

Hops
2 oz. Nugget leaf hops
2 oz. Galena leaf hops
1 oz. Cascade hops

Other

1 oz. Amylase enzyme

Yeast 2 packs Doric ale yeast

Procedure Put grains into two gallons water and boil. When a pot reaches boil, remove grains. Add dry extract and stir. Add hopped extract and licorice. Add Nugget, and Galena hops. Boil 70 minutes. This was a big thick mess and needs a big pot---mine boiled over. Add Cascade for finishing. Cool and pitch yeast and amylase. Put in a big fermenter with a blow tube---my batch blew the cover creating a marvelous mess all over the wall. Eventually rack to secondary and ferment a long time (at least 3 weeks).

Cream of Oats Stout

Category Stout
Recipe Type All Grain

Fermentables

6 lbs. Klages 2-row pale malt
.5 lbs. Dextrin malt 1-1/8 lbs. Rolled oats
.5 lbs. Crystal malt
.5 lbs. Chocolate malt
.25 lbs. Roasted barley

Hops

1 oz. Clusters boiling hops (7.4 alpha)
.5 oz. Cascade hops

Other

10 oz. Lactose
.5 tsp Irish moss

Yeast Wyeast #1007: German ale

Procedure Mash in 3 quarts cold water. Raise temperature to 153 degrees and hold until iodine test indicates complete conversion. Transfer to lauter turn and sparge to yield 7 gallons. Boil 1 hour, adding boiling hops. Add finishing hops and Irish moss in last 10 minutes. Sparge, cool and pitch yeast.

Dark of the Moon Cream Stout

Category Stout
Recipe Type Extract

Fermentables
5 lbs. Dry dark malt extract
2 lbs. Crystal malt 40L
1.5 lbs. Crystal malt 20L
12 oz. Chocolate malt
4 oz. Roasted barley

Hops
.5 oz. Eroica hops (20 BU)
.25 oz. Chinook hops (12 BU)
.75 oz. Nugget hops (12 BU) (subst. N. Brewer (? BU))
1 oz. Cascade hops (5 BU)
1 oz. Eroica hops (4 BU)

Other
6 oz. dextrin powder
.5 tsp calcium carbonate

Yeast Wyeast #1098 British Ale yeast

Procedure Made a yeast starter 3 days before pitching. Used 2 tablespoons DME and 1 cup water. Next time use 2 cups water. Crack all grains and steep for 30 minutes at about 160 degrees along with the calcium carbonate. Strain out grains and sparge into about 2-1/2 gallons pre-boiled water. Total boil about 5 gallons. Add dry malt and dextrin and bring to a boil. Add 1/2 ounce of Eroica and 1/4 ounce of Chinook when boil starts. 30 minutes later add 3/4 ounce Nugget hops. Chill with an immersion chiller. Rack to a carboy, fill to 5 gallons and let sit overnight to allow the trub to settle out. The next morning rack it to a plastic primary, pitched the yeast starter, and add the 1 ounce of Cascades and Eroica hops

Double Party Chocolate Stout

Category Stout
Recipe Type Extract
A double chocolate stout with a strong cocoa flavor. Color is dark brown, and the aroma is that of cocoa.

Fermentables
6.0 Lbs. Light Dry Malt Extract
0.333 Lbs. Roasted Barley
0.667 Lbs. Chocolate Malt
0.333 Lbs. 60 L Crystal Malt
0.5 Lbs. Carapils Malt

Hops
3.0 oz. East Kent Goldings (4.0% AA) 60 minutes
1.0 oz. UK Fuggles (4.0% AA) 30 minutes
1.0 oz. UK Fuggles (4.0% AA) 1 minute

Other
1.0 Lbs. Baker's Chocolate
1.0 Tbsp Irish Moss
Yeast White Labs' Irish Ale (WLP 004)

Procedure 1) Steep crushed grains in 5 gallons of 150 F water for 30 minutes. Remove grains and bring water to a boil. 2) Melt chocolate in a double boiler and add to boiling water stirring constantly. 3) Dissolve DME in boiling water, let boil for 15 minutes. 4) Add boiling hops for 60 minutes of the boil. 5) Add flavor hops for 30 minutes of the boil. 6) Add Irish moss for the final 15 minutes of the boil. 7) Steep 1 oz. of aroma hops for a minute after turning off the heat on the water. 8) Cool wort and add to fermenter to pitch the yeast. 9) Primary fermentation was 5 days, and secondary fermentation was 10 days. A layer of oil will be present at the top of the fermenting beer, try not to transfer this during any transfer step you have.

Double Stout

Category Stout
Recipe Type Extract

Fermentables
10 lbs. Dark malt extract
1 lb. Black patent malt
2 lbs. Crystal malt
.5 lbs. Flaked barley
.25 lbs. Roasted barley
.5 stick licorice

Hops
2 1/2 Bullion hops
1 1/2 Kent Golding hops

Other
3 gallons water   1 tsp ascorbic acid
.5 tsp citric acid 1 tsp Irish moss

Yeast 3/4 ounce ale yeast (three standard packages)

Procedure Combine water, dark malt extract, and Bullion
hop. Boil for 20 minutes. Add black patent malt through Irish
moss. Boil for 5 minutes. Remove from heat and add Kent
Golding hops. Steep for 5 minutes. Cool and add yeast
nutrient and ale yeast. When fermentation has "stopped", add
priming sugar and bottle.

Drowsy Duck Imperial Stout

Category Stout
Recipe Type All Grain

Fermentables
11 lb.. (5kg) British pale ale malt
1 lb. (450g) crystal malt, 120L

8 oz. (225g) chocolate malt
2 lb. (900g) dark brown sugar

Hops

20 HBUs Fuggles, 60 minutes   5 HBUs Kent Golding, 10 minutes

Yeast Wyeast Irish Ale (#1084)

Procedure Bring 4 gallons (15l) water to 140F (60C) and add malts. Stir slowly until grist is completely mixed into water. Add gypsum or calcium carbonate to adjust mash pH to 5.0 (to 5.3) if needed. Bring mash to 150F (65C) and stir thoroughly. Stir every 15 minutes and reheat to 150F (65C) every 30 minutes (starch conversion). After two hours, bring mash to 170F (77C) for 10 minutes. Sparge with 3 gallons (11l) 170F (77C) water.

Boil 30 minutes and add hops. Boil for another hour, adding finishing hops 10 minutes before end of boil.

Chill to 50F, (10C) rack to secondary. Twelve to fourteen hours later, rack wort off trub and measure SG. Reserve and freeze wort equivalent to 6oz. (340g) sugar for priming, and pitch yeast starter in the rest.

Rack to carboy when primary fermentation is done and settle yeast out with is in glass. Prime with thawed gyle and bottle.

Dry Rye Stout

Category Stout
Recipe Type All Grain

Fermentables   8 lbs. 2 row malt
1.1 lb. Flaked rye

.5 lb cara-pils malt
.75 lb roast barley
.25 lb black patent malt
.25 lb chocolate malt
.25 lb crystal malt [80L]

Hops

3 oz. Fuggles leaf hops [4.2%- for 60 min. ->12.6 HBU] 1 oz. Goldings leaf hops [5.2%- for 10 min.->0 HBU]

Other
1 pinch Irish moss

Yeast WYeast London Ale[1028]--starter made from new packet

Procedure Grind all grains and place them into the mash. Mash in at 71C (160F). The temperature should drop to 66C (152F). Mash for 2.5 hrs at 66C (152F). Mash out for 5 min at 76C (169F). Sparge 6gal @71-76C (160F-169F). Boil for 1 hour. 3 oz. of Fuggles for 60 minutes. 1 oz. of Goldings and Irish moss for last 10 minutes Cool, remove trub, and pitch.

Ferment at room temperature 20C (68F) until fermentation ceases. About 10 days. A single stage fermentation was used. Then bottle or keg as desired (I kegged it).

Eliminator Stout
Category Stout
Recipe Type Partial Mash

Fermentables
1.0 Lbs. Clover Honey
7.0 Lbs. Dark Malt
0.5 Lbs. Roasted Barley 1190-13m

0.5 Lbs. Crystal barley 120L
0.5 Lbs. Flaked oats
0.5 Lbs. Flaked barley

Hops
2.0 oz. Fuggles Hops (finish)
1.0 oz. Northern Brewer Hops (boil)

Other
2.0 Tsp gypsum

Yeast Irish Yeast Y108-4

Procedure Add roasted barley & crystal malt to cold water and slowly bring to a boil. After 20 minutes, remove grain. Add honey, malt, flaked oats, barley, gypsum, and boiling hops. Boil for 15 minutes, then removes finishing hops. Cool wort, add to 5 gallon mark on your bucket. When your wort is cool, at 75 degrees, add yeast.

Finster's Finest Chocolate Raspberry Stout

Category Stout
Recipe Type Extract

Fermentables
3.3 lbs. John Bull plain dark extract syrup
3 lbs. Plain dry malt extract
1 lb. Crystal malt
.5 lbs. Roasted barley
.5 lbs. Black patent malt
3 lbs. Frozen raspberries
1-1/4 cups dry malt extract

Hops
1.5 oz. Northern Brewer hops pellets
.5 oz. Willamette hops pellets

Other
Gypsum to create hard water 8 oz. Baker's chocolate

Yeast 2 packages Edme dry ale yeast

Procedure Heat 1.5 gal water to 170F. Add grains, cover, and let sit for 30 min. stirring occasionally. Remove grains. Bring to boil. Add gypsum, malt extracts, NB hops, chocolate, and boil for 60 min. Turn off heat. Add raspberries to hot wort (be careful of splashing). Cover, and let sit for 13 min. Add Willamette hops. Cover, and let sit for 2 min. Cool wort. Dump entire mess into primary, aerate, and pitch yeast (I rehydrated it while waiting for the rasp. to steep in wort). 4-5 days in primary. Rack *very carefully* into secondary, to avoid racking fruit particles. 10-14 days in secondary (I went 14).

First Oatmeal Stout

Category Stout
Recipe Type Extract

Fermentables
6 lb unhopped dark malt extract
1 lb unhopped dry malt
8 oz. Chocolate malt
6 oz. Roasted barley
 4 oz. Black patent malt
8 oz. Rolled oats
Hops
2 oz. Northern Brewer - 8.2 AAU
2 oz. Fuggles - 4.2 AAU

Other
1 tbs CaCO3   Irish Moss - 30 min

Yeast Liquid Irish Ale yeast

Procedure I cracked the grains using my food processor in short bursts (worked great!). Transferred them in a mesh strainer and shook to remove dust. I did this outside so as not to contaminate the kitchen. These were then placed with the oats (ungrounded) into a grain bag. I preheated a 10 qt. (12-pack) cooler with boiling water, added the grain bag and 175 deg. water. Water cooled to the target of 160 deg. and steeped for 15 minutes. Things were working beautifully. I boiled the water and added the extract, CaCO3 and the steep liquor. This is where I have the question.

In previous extract/grain batches I have steeped grains, then washed them in some of the unboiled water until the water ran "clear." I started to do this with the black/chocolate malts but obviously with the black grains it wouldn't have run clear.

Eventually, the water I was using started to become the consistency of thin syrup. If I continued to wash them I would have been there for days until the liquid began to thin and probably would have ended up with 10 gallons of wort.

Grapefruit Taste

Category Stout
Recipe Type Extract

Fermentables

9 lb "Dutch" amber dry malt extract
1 lb Medium Brown Sugar
.5 lb roasted barley
.5 lb chocolate barley

Hops

4 oz. Northern Brewer hop pellets AA 8.8%
2 oz. Cascade hop pellets AA 5.4%

Other

1 inch of brewers liquorish 1 tsp Irish moss

Yeast Wyeast #1084 Irish Ale yeast

Procedure I steeped roasted/chocolate barley in 1 gal 160 deg F water for 30 min, strained into kettle, and sparged with 1/2 gal 170 deg F water. Added an additional gal of water and brought to a boil. Removed from heat and dissolved extract and sugar, returned to burner and brought to boil. Added liquorish and Northern Brewer hops. Added Irish moss at 45 min. Boiled for 55 min and then added Cascade hops. Boiled for additional 5 min and cooled in ice water bath. (total boil 60 minutes).

Strained cooled wort into 2.5 gal of previously boiled and cooled water in primary fermenter (6.7 gal plastic, closed fermentation).O.G. 1.078. Pitched yeast directly from a smack pack at 78 deg F. Active fermentation noticeable after 12 hours. Primary fermentation was at approx 72 deg for five days. Racked to secondary (5 gal glass) S.G 1.042, tasted fruity but not overpowering. After 13 days total, all fermentation activity ceased. Bottled with 3/4 cup honey. F.G. 1.030.

Joan's Potholder Oatmeal Stout

Category Stout
Recipe Type All Grain

Fermentables

5 lbs. 2--row pale malt
1.5 lbs. Steel cut oats
.5 lbs. Malted wheat
1.5 lbs. 80 L. Crystal malt
1 lb. Black patent malt
1 lb. Chocolate malt
1 lb. Roasted barley
.5 lbs. Cara-pils malt
3 lbs. Dark Australian DME

Hops

1 oz. Chinook pellets (13.6% alpha) (boil 60 minutes)
.5 oz. Perle pellets (8% alpha) (boil 35 minutes)
.25 oz. Hallertauer pellets (3% alpha) (boil 35 minutes)
.25 oz. Tettnanger pellets (3.4% alpha) (boil 35 minutes)
.75 oz. Hallertauer (steep for aroma)
.75 oz. Tettnanger (steep for aroma) 1 oz. Cascade (dry hop)

Other

.5 lbs. lactose 1 tsp Irish moss

Yeast Wyeast Irish ale yeast

Procedure Single-step infusion mash, partial mash recipe. Strike Temperature 170 into 12 liters of treated water, allow Burton on Trent. Note This was a little too thick, so use a little more water. Mashed for 45 minutes, 170 F. proteolysis step for 10 minutes. Sparged for almost two hours, while adding runoff to brew kettle to get boiling. Sparge SG ran from 1.09 down to about 1.025 when I had enough wort. Added 3 lbs. DME (Dark Australian) to bring wort to 1.06 SG. I added 8 oz. of lactose and a tsp. of dry moss before killing the fire.

I pitched a large starter of the Irish Wyeast strain and got lots of blow off. I had the extra wort in a 4 liter auxiliary. I used this to fill up the secondary after racking off the lees. Dry hopping was done in the secondary with the cascade. After 2 weeks, the SG was only down to 1.03, and fermentation was very slow.

Joan's Potholder Oatmeal Stout

Category Stout
Recipe Type All Grain
Fermentables
5 lbs. 2--row pale malt
1.5 lbs. Steel cut oats
.5 lbs. malted wheat
1.5 lbs. 80 L. Crystal malt
1 lb. Black patent malt
1 lb. Chocolate malt
1 lb. Roasted barley
.5 lbs. Cara-pils malt
3 lbs. Dark Australian DME

Hops
1 oz. Chinook pellets (13.6% alpha) (boil 60 minutes)
.5 oz. Perle pellets (8% alpha) (boil 35 minutes)
.25 oz. Hallertauer pellets (3% alpha) (boil 35 minutes)
.25 oz. Tettnanger pellets (3.4% alpha) (boil 35 minutes)

.75 oz. Hallertauer (steep for aroma)
.75 oz. Tettnanger (steep for aroma)
1 oz. Cascade (dry hop)

Other
.5 lbs. Lactose
1 tsp Irish moss

Yeast Wyeast Irish ale yeast

Procedure Single-step infusion mash, partial mash recipe. Strike Temperature 170 into 12 liters of treated water, allow Burton on Trent. Note This was a little too thick, so use a little more water. Mashed for 45 minutes, 170 F. proteolysis step for 10 minutes. Sparged for almost two hours, while adding runoff to brew kettle to get boiling. Sparge SG ran from 1.09 down to about 1.025 when I had enough wort. Added 3 lbs. DME (Dark Australian) to bring wort to 1.06 SG. I added 8 oz. of lactose and a tsp. of dry moss before killing the fire.

I pitched a large starter of the Irish Wyeast strain and got lots of blow off. I had the extra wort in a 4 liter auxiliary. I used this to fill up the secondary after racking off the lees. Dry hopping was done in the secondary with the cascade. After 2 weeks, the SG was only down to 1.03, and fermentation was very slow.

Klingon Stout

Category Stout
Recipe Type Extract

Fermentables
6.6 lb dark malt extract syrup
1 lb crushed crystal malt
.5 lb black patent malt

1/3 lb roasted barley
Hops
1.5 oz. Northern Brewers hops--boil 60 min.
1 oz. Tettnanger hops --finishing last 2 min.

Other
2 quarts prune juice WITH NO PRESERVATIVES!!!!
.75 c. Corn sugar to prime

Yeast ale yeast

Procedure Steep grains 30 min at 150F. Strain into brew pot and rinse with one gal hot water. Add extract, boiling hops and additional gal. water and boil 1 hr. Add finishing hops last 2 min. Turn off heat and add prune juice to pasteurize for 10 min (probably not necessary since the juice is already pasteurized). Pour into primary fermenter and top with cold water up to 5 gal. Pitch yeast when cool. Rack to secondary a week later. Bottle when ready. Age at least 4 week.

Pumpernickel Stout

Category Stout
Recipe Type All Grain

Fermentables
.5 lb crystal malt (I imagine this was 40 - 50^L)
3 oz. Black malt
1 lb lager malt, home roasted to light brown
3 lb. Lager malt
3 lb pale ale malt

Hops
.5 oz. Tetnanger hops for aroma
3 oz. Northern Brewer hops (no AA noted)

Other
.75 lb. Medium ground rye berries

6 oz. Quick oats

Yeast Red Star ale yeast

Procedure I corona milled the grains. Cook the rye meal and oatmeal with 1 gal water 45 minutes, ad for 2-1/2 gal strike temp water and rest of grains to achieve mash temp of ~150^F. I believe I must have mashed higher, like 153, since I got (and would want) a dextrinous wort. I am surprised to see from my notes that I mashed for 3 hrs., longer than I do now. I do (and did) this by putting my kettle in the oven at 150^F. Sparged 7 gal, had a little trouble with it is stuck, so I stirred and reset it; rye will do this, but roller milled malt should help), boiled 2 hrs to 5 gal. at 1.054 SG. Didn't note whether I boiled the hops all two hrs., probably just the last hour. Tetnanger for 10 min. steep after heat off. Counter current cooled, pitched with lots of (dry Red Star Ale) yeast from the previous secondary fermenter. Open fermenter, skimmed, racked after three days, still quite active (beer filled air lock once). I continued to bubble a long time, until I finally just bottled 4 oz. corn sugar a one month. No F.G. taken.

Drowsy Duck Imperial Stout

Category Stout
Recipe Type All Grain

Fermentables
11 lb.. (5kg) British pale ale malt
1 lb. (450g) crystal malt, 120L
8 oz. (225g) chocolate malt
2 lb. (900g) dark brown sugar

Hops
20 HBUs Fuggles, 60 minutes
5 HBUs Kent Golding, 10 minutes

Yeast Wyeast Irish Ale (#1084)

Procedure Bring 4 gallons (15l) water to 140F (60C) and add malts. Stir slowly until grist is completely mixed into water. Add gypsum or calcium carbonate to adjust mash pH to 5.0 (to 5.3) if needed. Bring mash to 150F (65C) and stir thoroughly. Stir every 15 minutes and reheat to 150F (65C) every 30 minutes (starch conversion). After two hours, bring mash to 170F (77C) for 10 minutes. Sparge with 3 gallons (11l) 170F (77C) water.

Boil 30 minutes and add hops. Boil for another hour, adding finishing hops 10 minutes before end of boil.

Chill to 50F, (10C) rack to secondary. Twelve to fourteen hours later, rack wort off trub and measure SG. Reserve and freeze wort equivalent to 6oz. (340g) sugar for priming, and pitch yeast starter in the rest.

Rack to carboy when primary fermentation is done and settle yeast out with isinglas. Prime with thawed gyle and bottle.

Dry Rye Stout

Category Stout
Recipe Type All Grain

Fermentables
8 lbs. 2 row malt
1.1 lb. Flaked rye
.5 lb cara-pils malt
.75 lb roast barley
.25 lb black patent malt
.25 lb chocolate malt
.25 lb crystal malt [80L]

Hops
3 oz. Fuggles leaf hops [4.2%- for 60 min. ->12.6 HBU]
1 oz. Goldings leaf hops [5.2%- for 10 min.->0 HBU]

Other
1 pinch Irish moss

Yeast WYeast London Ale[1028]--starter made from new packet

Procedure Grind all grains and place them into the mash. Mash in at 71C (160F). The temperature should drop to 66C (152F). Mash for 2.5 hrs at 66C (152F). Mash out for 5 min at 76C (169F). Sparge 6gal @71-76C (160F-169F). Boil for 1 hour. 3 oz. of Fuggles for 60 minutes. 1 oz. of Goldings and Irish moss for last 10 minutes Cool, remove trub, and pitch.

Ferment at room temperature 20C (68F) until fermentation ceases. About 10 days. A single stage fermentation was used. Then bottle or keg as desired (I kegged it).

First Oatmeal Stout

Category Stout
Recipe Type Extract

Fermentables

6 lb unhopped dark malt extract
1 lb unhopped dry malt
8 oz. Chocolate malt
 6 oz. Roasted barley
4 oz. Black patent malt
8 oz. Rolled oats

Hops
2 oz. Northern Brewer - 8.2 AAU
2 oz. Fuggles - 4.2 AAU

Other
1 tbs CaCO3   Irish Moss - 30 min

Yeast Liquid Irish Ale yeast

Procedure I cracked the grains using my food processor in short bursts (worked great!). Transferred them in a mesh strainer and shook to remove dust. I did this outside so as not to contaminate the kitchen. These were then placed with the oats (ungrounded) into a grain bag. I pre-heated a 10 qt. (12-pack) cooler with boiling water, added the grain bag and 175 deg. water. Water cooled to the target of 160 deg. and steeped for 15 minutes. Things were working beautifully. I boiled the water and added the extract, CaCO3 and the steep liquor. This is where I have the question.

In previous extract/grain batches I have steeped grains, then washed them in some of the unboiled water until the water ran "clear." I started to do this with the black/chocolate malts but obviously with the black grains it wouldn't have run clear. Eventually, the water I was using started to become the consistency of thin syrup. If I continued to wash them, I would have been there for days until the liquid began to thin and probably would have ended up with 10 gallons of wort..

CHAPTER 6- WHEAT BEERS

Dark Raspberry Wheat

Category Wheat Beer
Recipe Type Extract

Fermentables
3-4.5 lbs. Laaglander dark powdered malt extract
3 lbs. Dry or canned wheat extract
11 Each 12 oz. Cans Knudsens frozen Raspberry Nectar
concentrate

Hops
1.25 oz. Hallertauer Hops (boiling)
0.25 oz. Hallertauer Hops (finishing)
0.5 oz. Saaz Hops (finishing)

Other
1 tsp North Sea, Irish Moss

Yeast 1 pkg Munton and Fison Ale yeast

Procedure Be careful with this recipe. At all stages prior to bottling, it quite eager to escape from whatever container it is placed on including the wort pot. Combine grain extracts in your largest pot along with enough water to fill it 2/3 full (No more than 3 1/2 gals.) and boil for 45 mins. 30 mins before end of boil, add boiling hops and Irish moss. Add finishing hops 5 mins. before end of boil. Upon completion, place in primary fermentation container, add water to 4-4.25 gals. and allow to cool to 150 deg F. Add six cans of the Raspberry Nectar, cover and allow to cool to body temp before pitching yeast. After a couple of days, when the head subsides, add the other five cans of raspberry concentrate. (It really likes to go out the top at this stage.) In two or three more days, the head should again subside, at which time it should be racked into a glass carboy with a minimum of head space. Follow the progress of fermentation. When the ring of bubbles disappears at the neck of the carboy, it is time to bottle. Rack and combine with 3/4 cup of corn sugar (dissolved in a minimum of boiling water) and bottle. It should be ready in three to four weeks from bottling time, which makes it the fastest wine that I've ever made, if it can be said to be such. Personally, I think it's the best too.

Gelber Weizen

Category Wheat Beer
Recipe Type Extract

Fermentables
6.0 Lbs. Weizen Dry Malt Extract
4.0 oz. Munich Malt

Hops
1.0 oz. Hallertauer Pellet (~4.4% AA)

Other
1.0 Pinch Irish Moss

Yeast Wyeast #3333 German Wheat Yeast

Procedure Add 4oz. Munich Malt to a grain sack and steep in 1/2gal. Water as you bring to boil. This takes approximately 20min. Once to a boil, remove grain sack and strain the liquid into the brew pot. Sparge the grains with 3/2gal. hot water and add to the brew pot. Add an additional 1/2gal. Water and bring to a boil. Add 6lbs. DME and 1oz. hops and boil for 60min, adding a pinch of Irish Moss with 10min. left. Remove brew pot and chill. Strain into the primary fermenter and add cold water to make 5gal. Let cool until below 75degreesF and pitch yeast. After about 4 days (or when fermentation slows) rack into a secondary fermenter. *optional* Now might be a good time to clarify the batch by soaking 1/2tsp. gelatin finings in cold water for an hour, then boiling to dissolve. Mix this solution into the secondary fermenter after racking. After about 14 days (or when fermentation stops) bottle with 5/4cup Weizen DME boiled in 1pint of water for 5min. Primary and Secondary fermentation is optimum around 73degreesF.

German Hefe Weizen

Category Wheat Beer
Recipe Type All Grain

Fermentables
15 lbs. Ireks Wheat Malt
10.5 lbs. DeWolf-Cosyns Pils Malt

Hops
2 oz. 4.6% German Hallertauer Pellets (assume 25% utilization) 60 min

Yeast Weihenstephan Weizan Yeast (96? 69?)

Procedure Pre-boil all water, chill, and siphon off the sediment. Mash in at 99F, hold for 15 minutes.
Boost to 122F, hold for 15 minutes.

Perform first decoction with thickest 40% of the mash. Heat in 15 minutes to 160F, hold 15 minutes. Heat in 15 minutes to boiling. Boil for 20 minutes. Mix back into mash turn over 10 minutes.

Hold at 147F for 20 minutes.

Perform second decoction with 30% of the mash. Heat in 15 minutes to 160F, hold 15 minutes. Heat in 15 minutes to boiling. Boil for 10 minutes. Mix back into mash turn over 10 minutes.

Sparge at 172F to collect 15 gallons. Boil two hours. After hot break occurs collect one gallon of species (wort) for priming.

Add hops for last 60 minutes.

Pitch yeast at 58F. Allow temperature to rise to 65F over three days.
Bottle with 1 4/5 qts species per 5 gallons..

Puppy's Surprise Spiced Wheat Ale
Category Wheat Beer
Recipe Type All Grain

Fermentables
3 lb. (1.35kg) Belgian pale malt
5 lb. (2.25kg) Belgian wheat malt
2 lb. (900g) rolled oats
0.5c (120ml) corn sugar

Hops
3 HBUs Styrian Golding hops (60 minute boil)
1.5 HBUs Styr. Golding hops (30 minute boil)
0.5 oz. (14g) Kent Golding hops (finish)

Other
0.5 oz. (14g) sweet orange peel (30 minute boil)
0.25 oz. (7g) sweet orange peel (10 minute boil)
0.75 oz. (21g) crushed coriander (finish)
Gypsum or calcium carbonate

Yeast Wyeast Weihenstephen (#3068)

George Braun

Procedure Boil oats in 3 gallons (11l) water until gelatinized. Replace lost volume with cold water and adjust temperature to 125F (52C). Add malts. Stir slowly until grist is completely mixed into water. Measure pH and adjust to 5.3 with gypsum.

Heat to 130F (55C) if temperature has fallen too low and rest at this temperature 45 minutes, stirring every 15 and boosting temperature as needed.

Boost temperature to 150F (65C) and rest 2 hours, stirring every 15 minutes and heating to 150F (65C) every 30 minutes.

Sparge with 4 gallons (15l) water, pH 5.7, 170F (75C).

Boil 30 minutes and add first hop aliquot. Boil another 30 minutes and add the second and add the first aliquot of orange peel (pre- soak peel in water if dried). Boil another 20 minutes and add a second aliquot of orange peel. Add finishing spices at end of boil and sit 15 minutes on the stove, flame off.

Chill to 50F (10C) and rack into secondary. Sit overnight and rack wort off trub in the morning. Wort pH should be between 5.0 and
5.3 at pitching. Pitch yeast.

Rack to carboy when primary fermentation is done and add isinglass. Settle 4-5 days.

Prime with sugar and bottle.

Tyson's Hefeweisen Amber
Category Wheat Beer
Recipe Type Extract

Fermentables

10.0 oz. "Special B" (60L) ground caramel malt
4.0 Lbs. Dry Amber Malt Extract
3.3 Lbs. Wheat Extract Syrup

Hops
2.0 oz. E.K.G. Hops (6.1%)

Other
5.0 Gallons Pre-boiled, purified water (Split 3 & 2)

Yeast White Labs #WL300, or preferred Hefeweisen Ale yeast

Procedure Steep caramel malt in 3 gallons hot (180+ degrees, but not boiling) water for 10 minutes with steeping sock, squeezing most of moister out before throwing out. Put over high heat, adding and dissolving dry malt and syrup before boiling starts, stirring to prevent clumping and settling. Bring to boil, stirring occasionally, and preventing over-boil. After 30 minutes of boil, add 1 oz. of hops. Stir and boil for another 20 minutes (50 total from beginning) and then add the other 1 oz. of hops. Boil for 10 more minutes, for a total of 60 min. boil. Cool to 80F degrees and add remaining 2 gal. pre-boiled purified water at room temp. Pitch yeast at 76-80F degrees. Primary fermentation should take 10 days at about 74F degrees (remember airlock, dark place, etc...) Recommend bottling over kegging. Secondary fermentation (for bottles) could take as few as 7 days, but 14 days are recommended. Serve cold. 7% Alc.

Wheat Berry
Category Wheat Beer
Recipe Type Extract

Fermentables
5-1/2 lbs. Light dried wheat malt extract
24 to 36 oz. Frozen raspberries
16 oz. Frozen blackberries

Hops
1-1/2 oz. Hallertauer or Northern Brewer (boiling), 7 HBU
.5 oz. Hallertauer Hersbrucker (finishing), 2-3 HBU

Other
1 tsp vanilla extract

Yeast Belgian ale yeast (Wyeast 1214)

Procedure Boil 2-1/2 gallons of water, add malt extract and boiling hops, and boil for 55-60 minutes. Turn off heat, add finishing hops, cool to 190 F and add the frozen fruit and vanilla. Let sit covered for 20 minutes, maintaining temperature at about 170 F and stirring occasionally. Cool to below 100F, add to carboy pre-filled with 2-1/2 gallons of water, straining out and pressing the fruit to extract most of the juice. Pitch the yeast, ferment at 70-72F, transfer to secondary after two days, then ferment completely out (about another 7 days). Prime with 3/4 cup corn sugar and bottle.

24 oz. of raspberries gives a fairly subtle beer, with a mild tart raspberry underpinning that all of my friends loved. 36 oz. of berries give a more assertive, but not overwhelming, raspberry flavor. Note that Belgian ale yeast will give stronger "clove" overtones when fermented at temperatures of 75-78F, and milder flavors at 70-72F.

CHAPTER 7- ESB

Jeff's ESB Extra Special Basenji Bitter
Category ESB
Recipe Type All Grain

Fermentables

2 lbs. British Crystal Cracked Grains
6 lbs. Dutch Amber Dry Malt Extract
1 Cup English Light Dry Malt Extract (for priming)

Hops
1.5 oz. Cascade Hops (finishing hops)
.5 oz. Cascade Hops (for hop tea at bottling)
2.25 oz. Northern Brewer Hops (for brewing)

Other
2 tsp Sparkolloid (last 15 minutes of boil)
2 tsp Irish Moss (last 30 minutes of boil)

Yeast 1 pkg. CWE A6 Dry Yeast

Easy Beer Brewing : Brewers Recipe Guide for Beginners is the definitive book for novice in beer brewing at home, this book has something for you. This book also includes recipes and guidelines. Everything you need to know how to get started is here. Including classic and new recipes for brewing wheat's, lagers, stouts, ales, and fruits. And using the basic ingredients like malts, hops, yeast and water. And much, much more.

Procedure Put British Crystal cracked grains in straining bag and add to 2 gal. cold water. Heat to boil, removing grains just before boil starts. Sparge grains. Add Dutch Amber DME. Boil 1 hour. Add Northern Brewer in straining bag to wort. Boil. Add Cascade finishing hops 1 minute before end of boil. Remove from heat and let hops steep for 10 minutes. Sparge. Make a starter from 1 cup wort and 1 cup water, add yeast. Add enough water to top off to 5 gals. Pitch starter. Ferment for 1 week. Rack to carboy for 3 weeks. At bottling, siphon out 2 cups of beer and warm on stove. Dissolve English Light DME into hot beer and bring to boil. Add 1/2 oz. Cascade hops and steep for 10 minutes. Pour primer in bottling bucket and siphon carboy into the bucket. Bottle. Let bottle condition for 3 weeks.

Red Hook ESB Clone

Category ESB
Recipe Type All Grain

Fermentables
3500 Grams Klages Two-Row Malt
575 grams Toasted Klages Two-Row Malt (Toast at 375F for 15 minutes)
225 Grams Crystal Malt 60L
500 Grams Cara-Pils Dextrine Malt

Hops
65 grams 4.6% Alpha Willamette Whole Hops (60 min)
20 Grams 4.6% Alpha Willamette Whole Hops (20 min)
40 Grams 3.9% Alpha Tettnanger Whole Hops (10 min)

Yeast Sierra Nevada cultured yeast or Wyeast #1098 British Ale yeast

Procedure Use a one step infusion mash (Adjust water according to local conditions). Mash in at 145F, then raise mash to 156F for starch conversion. Hold at 156F for 75 minutes, boost to 168F and mash out for 10 minutes. Sparge with sufficient water at 165F to yield 6.5 gallons of wort. I keep the mash temp on the high side to leave some residual roundness in the finished product, and the Crystal give the beer a hint of sweetness.

Boil entire volume of wort for 90+ minutes, adding hops as indicated. Force chill to pitching temperature (app. 70F). Ferment at 64-68F for 6 days in primary, then rack to secondary for 14-21 days. Prime according to personal preference. I use either 1/2 cup dextrose in 1 pint of water or 3/4 cup Light DME.

Trolleyman

Category ESB
Recipe Type Extract

Fermentables
6.6 lbs. Alexander light malt extract syrup
10 oz. 60 degree Lovibond crystal malt (crushed)
4 oz. malto-dextrin

Hops
32 IBU Willamette hop pellets (boil)
1.0 oz. Tettnang hop pellets (finish)
1.0 oz. Tettnang hop pellets (dry hop)

Other
1 tsp Irish moss
.75 cup corn sugar for priming

Yeast Wyeast # 1098 (British ale) liquid yeast

Procedure Steep crystal malt in 4 gallons 160 degree water for 30 minutes and strain out grains. Bring water to boil and add malt extract syrup, malto-dextrin and Willamette hops for a 60 minute boil. Add Irish moss for last 30 minutes of boil and add Tettnang hops for the last two minutes of boil.

Turn off heat and allow to steep for 30 minutes while chilling your wort. Transfer to primary, top off to 5 gallons and pitch yeast at 72 degrees.

Rack to secondary and add 1 oz. Tettnang hop pellets as dry hop. Add appropriate clarifiers, add 3/4 cup corn sugar and bottle.

CHAPTER 8- STEAM BEERS

Anchor Steam-Style Amber

Category Steam Beer
Recipe Type Extract

Fermentables
7 lbs. John Bull plain light malt extract
1/4-1/2 lbs. Crystal malt

Hops
2 oz. Northern Brewer hops (11 alpha) (boil)
1 oz. Cascade hops (5.6 alpha) (finish)

Yeast 2 packs lager yeast

Procedure Pour 1 gallon water into brew pot. Crush grains and add to brew pot. Bring to boil. Remove grains. Add malt extract. Add 1/3 of the boiling hops. After 20 minutes, add another 1/3 of hops. After another 20 minutes, add the last 1/3 of hops. After another 20 minutes, remove from heat and add finishing hops. Cover wort. Pour 3 gallons cold water into fermenter. Strain wort into fermenter along with enough water to make 5-1/2 gallons. Pitch yeast and put in blow off tube or airlock.

Batch #10 Gary's Oregon Steam Beer

Category Steam Beer
Recipe Type Extract

Fermentables
7 lbs. Amber malt extract
1 lb 20L Chrystal malt
.75 cup corn sugar (bottling)

Hops

1 1/2 oz. Cluster hops (boiling)
.5 oz. Cluster hops (finishing)

Yeast 1 package Wyeast California (2112)

Procedure Starter made 2 days ahead instead of one. Steep grains for 30 minutes. Sparge into kettle. Boil extract and hops for 60 minutes.

Desert Storm American Steam Beer
Category Steam Beer
Recipe Type All Grain

Fermentables
5 lbs. Klages lager malt
4 lbs. Pale Ale malt
1 lb. Crystal malt (40 or 60 deg Lovibond)

Hops
1.5 oz. Northern Brewer (alpha 8.0)
1.5 oz. Hallertauer (alpha 4.1)

Other
.5 tsp Irish moss

Yeast MeV High Temp Lager liquid yeast

Procedure Mash grains for 25 minutes at 125 degrees and 90 minutes at 150 degrees. Mash-out for 10 minutes at 168 degrees. Sparge. Bring to boil and add Northern Brewer hops. Boil 60 minutes. At the last minute toss in Hallertauer. Cool. Pitch yeast.

Ginger Steamer

Category Steam Beer
Recipe Type Extract

Fermentables
6 lb unhopped Amber liquid extract
1 lb 120L Carmel Malt
1/2 lb Victory Malt (25L) (Oven Toasted at 350F for 15 min)
1/2 lb Double Malt (45L)

Hops
.5 oz. Cascade (15 min left)
.5 oz. Cascade (7 min left)
1 oz. Chinook 13.6 % (Boil)
.5 oz. Cascade (2 min steep)
.5 ounce Cascade (dry hop in secondary)

Other
1 oz. fresh Ginger indiscriminately put in the last few
minutes of the boil (15 min left)

Yeast Wyeast's California yeast

Steam Beer

Category Steam Beer
Recipe Type Extract

Fermentables
6.6 lbs. American Classic light malt extract
.5 lbs. Crystal malt (10 L.)
. 5 lbs. crystal malt (20 L.)
.5 cup honey (priming)

Hops
1.5 oz. Tettnanger hops (60 minute boil)

.25 oz. Tettnanger (30 minute boil)
.75 oz. Hallertauer hops (30 minute boil)
.25 oz. Tettnanger (10 minute boil)
.25 oz. Hallertauer (10 minute boil)
1 oz. Kent Golding hops (dry hop)

Other
 1 tsp., salt
1.5 tsp., gypsum

Yeast Wyeast Steam beer yeast

Procedure Crack the crystal malt and add to 1 gallon of water and bring to a boil then strain off the wort. Add the extract and return to a boil. Add the hops at the given times. Cool wort and pitch yeast.

Sour Mash
Category Sour Mash
Recipe Type All Grain

Fermentables
5 lbs. 2--row Klages (mash @ 158 for 14 hours)
10 lbs. wheat malt
10 lbs. 2--row Klages (infusion mash @155 for 1--1/2 hours)
2 lbs. wheat malt

Hops
2 oz. Centennial hops (12% alpha)

Other
.5 oz. Coriander (freshly crushed, added to fermenter)

Yeast yeast

Procedure Notes: I sour 1/2 (one half) of the mash, the high % wheat half, the other is straight infusion. I do however make an effort to minimize heat loss by using an ice chest and sealing the lid with duct tape. If it smells rotten, it is OK. The bacteria at work are for the most part aerobic. If it looks bad, it's OK. After 14 hours no matter how bad you think you screwed up, it's OK, just see the thing through, it is worth it.

Combine mashes for mash out @ 170F for 15 min. Sparge @ 170F. Boil for 75 minutes, then cool and split into two carboys. Pitch a Chimay culture into one and a Chico ale yeast into the other. Add 1/4 ounce freshly crushed coriander to each. After 7 days fermentation, blend the two batches together in a larger vessel. Ferment 7 days longer. Keg with 1/4 cup corn sugar per 5 gallons. Counter pressure bottled after 2 weeks.

Sourdough Beer

Category Sour Mash
Recipe Type Extract

Fermentables
2.75 lbs. Hopped light extract
.5 lbs. Pale malt
2 oz. Crystal malt (40 L.)
2 oz. Wheat malt
1.5 cups sourdough starter (wheat flour

Hops
.5 oz. Hallertauer hops

Yeast ale yeast

Procedure Dissolved extract in hot water, cooled and added starter. Let rest covered for 24 hours. Crushed and mashed grains. Poured liquid off sourdough sediment and strained into the wort. Boiled 1 hour and added hops at 40 minute mark. (Foul smelling boil!). Cooled and added ale yeast. Ferment as usual.

Anchor Steam-Style Amber

Category Steam Beer
Recipe Type Extract

Fermentables
7 lbs. John Bull plain light malt extract
1/4-1/2 lbs. Crystal malt

Hops

2 oz. Northern Brewer hops (11 alpha) (boil) 1 oz. Cascade hops (5.6 alpha) (finish)

Yeast 2 packs lager yeast

Procedure Pour 1 gallon water into **brew pot**. Crush grains and add to **brew pot**. Bring to boil. Remove grains. Add malt extract. Add 1/3 of the boiling hops. After 20 minutes, add another 1/3 of hops. After another 20 minutes, add the last 1/3 of hops. After another 20 minutes, remove from heat and add finishing hops. Cover wort. Pour 3 gallons cold water into fermenter. Strain wort into fermenter along with enough water to make 5-1/2 gallons. Pitch yeast and put in blow off tube or airlock.

Batch #10 Gary's Oregon Steam Beer

Category Steam Beer
Recipe Type Extract

Fermentables
7 lbs. Amber malt extract
1 lb 20L Chrystal malt
.75 cup corn sugar (bottling)

Hops
1 1/2 oz. Cluster hops (boiling)
.5 oz. Cluster hops (finishing)

Yeast 1 package Wyeast California (2112)

Procedure Starter made 2 days ahead instead of one. Steep grains for 30 minutes. Sparge into kettle. Boil extract and hops for 60 minutes.

Steam Beer

Category Steam Beer
Recipe Type Extract

Fermentables
6.6 lbs. American Classic light malt extract
.5 lbs. Crystal malt (10 L.)
.5 lbs. Crystal malt (20 L.)
.5 cup honey (priming)

Hops
1.5 oz. Tettnanger hops (60 minute boil)
.25 oz. Tettnanger (30 minute boil)
.75 oz. Hallertauer hops (30 minute boil)
.25 oz. Tettnanger (10 minute boil)
.25 oz. Hallertauer (10 minute boil)
1 oz. Kent Golding hops (dry hop)

Other
1 tsp., salt
1.5 tsp., gypsum
Yeast Wyeast Steam beer yeast

Procedure Crack the crystal malt and add to 1 gallon of water and bring to a boil then strain off the wort. Add the extract and return to a boil. Add the hops at the given times. Cool wort and pitch yeast.

Wit

Category Belgian Ale
Recipe Type Partial Mash

Fermentables
4 lbs. DeWolf-Cosyns "Pils" malt
3 lbs. Flaked (unmalted) wheat (cracked wheat works fine)
6 oz. Rolled oats
1 cup corn sugar (priming)

Hops
1 oz. Saaz hops (3.2% AA)

Other
1 oz. Bitter Curacao orange peel

.75 oz. Sweet orange or tangerine peel
.75 oz. Fresh ground coriander seed
.5 oz. Fresh ground anise seed A pinch of ground cumin
10 ml 88% food-grade lactic acid (at bottling)

Yeast BrewTek "Belgian Wheat" yeast

Procedure Dough-in grains with 3 gallons of soft water at
~90F. Protein rests:
30 minutes @ 117F 30 minutes @ 122F
30 minutes @ 126F (at this point, the wheat appears
dissolved) Pull first decoction; thickest third of the mash
Heat decoction to 160F, rest 15 minutes

Heat decoction to boiling, boil 15 minutes Return boiling
decoction to rest mash and stir.
Mash temperature should be near 145F. Rest 15 minutes. Pull
second decoction; thickest third of the mash

Heat decoction to 160F, rest 10 minutes   Heat decoction to boiling, boil 10 minutes Return boiling decoction to rest mash and stir. Mash temperature should be near 162F. Rest 15 minutes. Check starch. If not converted, rest longer.
Mash-out: 10 minutes @ 170F Sparge: 5 gallons @ 170F
Boil 60 minutes, adding hops at the beginning. Spices are added in the last 10 minutes of the boil or at knockout. I used a single- stage ferment (as I usually do). OG: 1.038. TG: 1.002.

Adding the lactic acid rather than biologically souring the beer is definitely a shortcut, and one that adds time to the processing, as it takes longer after bottling for the flavors to "marry" than for conditioning to develop. If you have a lactobacillus culture in your possession that will do the job, have at it.

CHAPTER 9- SPICED BEERS
Pumpkin Beer

Category Spiced Beers
Recipe Type All Grain

Fermentables
10 lb. American 2-row
.25 lb. Hickory Smoked Grains
.5 lb. Crystal Malt (40L)
.5 lb. Honey Malt (20-30L)
.5 lb. Dextrine Malt 1 oz. Chocolate Malt
.5 lb. Dark Brown Sugar
.5 several drops Lorann Pumpkin Oil

Hops
.25 oz. Cascade Hops (5.5AA) 60 minutes
.25 oz. Herzbrucker Hallertau Hops (2.2AA) 30 Minutes
.25 oz. Herzbrucker Hallertau Hops (2.2AA) 10 Minutes

Other

2 tsp. Cinnamon - 60 minutes
2 tsp Ginger - 60 minutes
2 tsp Allspice - 60 minutes
2 tsp Nutmeg - 60 minutes
6 Whole Whole Cloves - 60 minutes
1 tsp. Irish Moss - 30 minutes

Yeast ale yeast

Procedure Mash 3 gallons water at 142F. Add grains and stabilize at 132F for 20 minutes. Add 2 gallons boiling water to raise temp and stabilize at 158 for 45 minutes. Mash-out to 170F and sparge with 3 gallons 170F water. Boil down to 5.75 gallons. (My brew setup requires a little extra for assorted losses.)

Rauchbier

Category Spiced Beers
Recipe Type All Grain

Fermentables
10 lbs. Belgian Pils malt
1 lb. Smoked pale malt
.5 lb. 30L crystal malt
.75 cup corn sugar for priming

Hops
.75 oz. Bullion hops (boiling)
.75 oz. Hallertau hops (boiling)
.75 oz. Hallertau hops (added at end of boil)

Yeast Whitbread dry ale yeast

Procedure First, I smoked my malt on a barbeque grill. I built a frame out of wood and attached aluminum window screen to it. I then started a some coals and, when they were ready, put them on the grill with a few handfuls of wet hickory chips. I smoked 1 lb. Pale ale malt for 45 minutes - 1 hour and yes, it did get rather toasted by the heat, but I don't see that as a problem. I took the grain off the grill before it got roasted dark because I figured that would give it more of a porter-like flavor that I was not looking for.

My notes do not include a mashing schedule, but since my temperature control in my mashing setup isn't very good, it probably wouldn't do much good.

I used a very old package of Whitbread dry yeast as I had trouble with my Wyeast starter. It worked out OK, but I would suggest using Wyeast 1007 German Ale as I had originally intended.

Spiced Ale

Category Spiced Beers
Recipe Type Extract

Fermentables
7 lbs. Amber liquid extract (Alexander's
2 lbs. Crystal malt
1 lb. Chocolate malt cracked

Hops
2 oz. Hallertauer hops
2 oz. Saaz hops

Other
4 oz. Fresh ginger
2 tbsp ground cinnamon

Yeast Wyeast American Ale (Sierra Nevada?) Yeast 1 pint starter

Procedure Steep crystal and chocolate malt in hot, but not boiling, water for about 1/2 hour. Strain out grains, sparge with hot water. Add extract, stir until dissolved. Bring to a boil and add all the Hallertauer hops, the ginger and the cinnamon. Boil 1 hour. Chill the wort, transfer to primary, and add Saaz hops. Pitch the yeast. When the fermentation slows, transfer to secondary fermentor. Prime with 3/4 cup corn sugar and bottle when fermentation appears complete.

Sparky's After-Burner Brew

Category Spiced Beers
Recipe Type Extract

Fermentables
3.3 lbs. John Bull amber malt extract
.5 lbs. Crystal malt

.5 lbs. Dark dry malt
.5 lbs. Corn sugar

Hops
2 oz. Cascade hops

Other
10 ea fresh Jalapeno peppers

Yeast Munton & Fison ale yeast
Procedure Chop up Jalapeno peppers and boil them with the wort for 30 minutes or so. Strain them out when pouring wort into primary. Rack to secondary about 4 hours after pitching yeast.
Note: When handling jalapenos, be sure to wash hands thoroughly or wear rubber gloves. You'll find out why if you are a contact lens wearer. (I discovered this the hard way--- making pickles, not beer.)

Spiced Ale

Category Spiced Beers
Recipe Type Extract

Fermentables
7 lbs. Amber liquid extract (Alexander's
2 lbs. Crystal malt
1 lb. Chocolate malt cracked

Hops
2 oz. Hallertauer hops
2 oz. Saaz hops

Other
4 oz. Fresh ginger
2 tbsp ground cinnamon

Yeast Wyeast American Ale (Sierra Nevada?) Yeast 1 pint starter

Procedure Steep crystal and chocolate malt in hot, but not boiling, water for about 1/2 hour. Strain out grains, sparge with hot water. Add extract, stir until dissolved. Bring to a boil and add all the Hallertauer hops, the ginger and the cinnamon. Boil 1 hour. Chill the wort, transfer to primary, and add Saaz hops. Pitch the yeast. When the fermentation slows, transfer to secondary fermentor. Prime with 3/4 cup corn sugar and bottle when fermentation appears complete.

Spiced Brown Ale

Category Spiced Beers
Recipe Type Extract

Fermentables
7 lbs. Dark Munton & Fison malt extract syrup (2 cans)
.5 lbs. Crystal malt
1 lb. chocolate malt

Hops
1 oz. Fuggles pellet hops -- boil
1 oz. Fuggles pellet hops -- 15 minutes before end of boil
1 oz. Willamette pellet hops -- finish

Other
1 nutmeg, grated -- 15 minutes before end of boil
1 oz. Sliced ginger root -- 15 minutes before end

Yeast Whitbread ale dry yeast in a 20 oz. starter

Procedure Grain steeped in a colander in 2 gallons of cold water and brought to boiling: grain removed when boiling began. Some hops and spices allowed to pour into carboy. My notes don't mention fermentation times, so I would guess 1 to

1--1/2 weeks in primary, 2 weeks in secondary as a rough estimate.

Spiced Chili Beer

Category Spiced Beers
Recipe Type Extract

Fermentables
5 lbs. M&F light dry malt extract (unhopped)
.75 c. Corn sugar for priming

Hops
1 oz. Cascade pelletized hops (6.2% AA)

Other
6 each Chinese (Szechwan?) chilies
8 each chilies used for dry spicing (6 steamed, 2 unsteamed)

Yeast 1 pkg Yeast Lab Whitbread Ale Yeast

Procedure Removed stems and seed from chilies. Boiled extract and hops in ~3 gallons of water for 1 hour. Steeped chilies for 10 minutes, then discarded them. Started yeast in a small yeast starter. Pitched when wort cooled (I don't have a wort chiller). Bottled approx. 10 days later with priming sugar.

Before bottling I used a wine thief to taste the beer. Since the heat from the chilies was low I decided to steam a few chilies and "dry spice" in the bottle. I also made two bottles with unsteamed chilies. I'm not going to throw the chilies in the brew pot again. The very little spice was contributed from the six chilies I stopped.

I'll not put one chilies in each bottle again, either. Fortunately, I limited this to 8 beers. The steamed chilies made the brew overpowering. The unsteamed chilies were worse, with a mild infection that caused those beers to become hazy. The problem is not the heat. The dry spiced bottles are about as hot as Pace hot salsa. It's the Chile aroma that makes the beer undrinkable.

My next attempt will utilize dry spicing in the fermenter. I'll try 6 to 8 steamed chilies in a muslin bag. Also, I'll put more hops in the boil (1.5 oz. of similar bittering hops). The chilies seem to provide heat and aroma, which leaves flavor wide open to bittering.

Spicy Xmas Beer

Category Spiced Beers
Recipe Type Extract

Fermentables
3.3 lbs. Northwestern light malt extract
2 lbs. Dark malt extract
2 lbs. Wildflower honey

Hops
2 oz. Hertsburger hops (boil)
.5 oz. Goldings hops (finish)

Other
2 oz. Grated ginger (boil)
1 oz. Grated ginger (finish)

Yeast 2 packs Munton & Fison ale yeast

Procedure Start yeast. Boil malt extract, honey, boiling hops and boiling ginger for about 1 hour. Strain. Add finishing hops and ginger. Cool rapidly in tub. Pitch started yeast. Ferment. Prime and bottle.

Spicy Xmas Beer

Category Spiced Beers
Recipe Type Extract

Fermentables
3.3 lbs. Northwestern light malt extract
2 lbs. Dark malt extract
2 lbs. Wildflower honey

Hops
2 oz. Hertsburger hops (boil)
.5 oz. Goldings hops (finish)

Other
2 oz. Grated ginger (boil)
1 oz. Grated ginger (finish)

Yeast 2 packs Munton & Fison ale yeast
Procedure Start yeast. Boil malt extract, honey, boiling hops and boiling ginger for about 1 hour. Strain. Add finishing hops and ginger. Cool rapidly in tub. Pitch started yeast. Ferment. Prime and bottle.

Spruce Beer

Category Spiced Beers
Recipe Type All Grain

Fermentables
10 lbs. American 2-row malt
.5 lb crystal 40 Lovibond
1/3 lb chocolate malt

Hops
1 oz. Cascade hops (aa=7. 6%, 60 minutes)

Other
1 pint fresh spruce growths (30 min.)

Yeast German Ale Yeast

Procedure I mashed all grains together and did a protein rest at 122 degrees for 30 minutes and then mashed at 148-152 degrees for 1 hour.

Spruce Juice

Category Spiced Beers
Recipe Type Extract

Fermentables
5 lbs. Premier Malt hopped light malt extract
1 lb. Dried light plain malt extract
1/8 lbs. Roasted barley

Hops
2 oz. Cascade hops

Other
20 oz. Cup loosely filled with blue spruce cuttings

Yeast Ale yeast
Procedure Bring extract and 1 1/2 gallons of water to boil. Add Cascade hops and boil for a total of 45 minutes. Rinse spruce cuttings, then toss into the wort for the final twelve minutes of the boil. Cool. Pitch yeast.

Vanilla Cream Ale

Category Spiced Beers
Recipe Type Extract

Fermentables
4.0 Lbs. Alexander's Pale Malt Extract
0.5 Lbs. Crushed Caramunich Malt

1.0 Lbs. Rice Solids
1.0 Lbs. Lactose

Hops
 1.25 oz. 4% AA Tettnanger (aroma)
 0.75 oz. 4% AA Tettnanger (boiling)

Other
 1.5 Tbsp Vanilla Extract
 1.0 Tsp Irish Moss

Yeast WLP001

Procedure Steep crush grains in a muslin bag in 6 gallons water for 30 minutes at 150 Fahrenheit. Remove grains and discard. Bring Water up to a boil. Dissolve rice solids, lactose, and LME. Let wort come to a boil again and add boiling hops. After 45 minutes, add Irish Moss. After an additional 10 minutes, add aroma hops and vanilla extract. Turn off the heat after a full 60 minutes of boiling, cool and pitch yeast.

Winterbrew

Category Spiced Beers
Recipe Type Extract

Fermentables
 7 lbs. Dark malt extract
1 lb. Crystal malt
.5 lb. Chocolate malt
.25 lb. Black Patent
1 lb. Honey (clover)

Hops
 1 1/2 oz. Helletaur hops (bittering)
.5 oz. Helletauer hops (finishing)

Other

4 tsp. Nutmeg
10 inch Cinnamon stick
1 lb. Baker's chocolate

Yeast 14 grams Australian ale yeast

Procedure The O.G. on my batch was a healthy 1.065, but as you probably have guessed...the final gravity wasn't anywhere near 0...which was good. It is the adjuncts and un**fermentables** in this batch that give it that special holiday/winter character. I will definitely try this batch again... but before next winter!

Winter's Tavern Winter Ale

Category Spiced Beers
Recipe Type Extract

Fermentables
7 lbs. Alexander's Pale Malt Extract
20 oz. Clover Honey
1 lb. British Cara-Pils
1 lb. Crystal (40L)
2 lbs. klages 2-row (for partial mash of cara-pils)
.25 lbs. Chocolate Malt

Hops
.5 oz. Chinook Pellets (12%) (60 minute boil)
.5 oz. Cascade Leaf (7%) (30 minute boil)
1 oz. Hersbrucker Plugs (2.9%) (30 minute boil)
.5 oz. Hersbrucker Plugs (10 minute steep)
.5 oz. Hersbrucker Plugs (2 minute steep)
.5 ounce Cascade Leaf (7%) (Dry hopped in secondary)

Other
3 ea 3" cinnamon sticks
1 tsp whole cloves

1 tsp ground Allspice
2 oz. Grated fresh ginger
6 pods cardamom - slightly crushed

Yeast Wyeast American Ale

Procedure Performed partial mash of cara-pils, crystal and klages as described in CJOHB. Added all other **Fermentables** and brought to a rolling boil. Added hops as indicated as well as all spices for the last 10 minutes of the boil. Cooled in ice bath for approximately 30 minutes before moving to bucket with 2 gallons cold water to reduce oxidation. Let sit for 1 hour and then racked off trub into primary. (Spices, etc. included in the primary fermenter.) Pitched approximately 1 liter yeast starter, attached blow-off tube and had a cold one.

Xmas Ale

Category Spiced Beers
Recipe Type Extract

Fermentables
 4 1/4 Australian light extract, malt (liquid)
.5 lbs. Crystal malt
.25 lbs. Chocolate malt
1/8 lbs. Flaked barley
.5 cup brown sugar

Hops
 2 1/2 Northern brewer hops
1 oz. Cascade (finishing)

Other
 .5 tsp cinnamon
1 tsp whole clove

Yeast Ale yeast

Procedure Add all the grain and malt into the water and boil. After it starts to boil, add Northern brewer and spices. After about 45 minutes, turn off heat, add the Cascade. After 20 minutes, filter into carboy. Pitch yeast when cool. Clarify and bottle in a week.

About The Author

George Braun is an experienced and respected brewer. With his in-depth knowledge and years of experience in beer brewing, he loves to help other brewers make great beer and expand their knowledge while enjoying the adventure at the same time. He always speaks from personal experience , humbly including any mistakes he has made to help others avoid making them too. He is a real treat to read.

Printed in October 2022
by Rotomail Italia S.p.A., Vignate (MI) - Italy